Crystal Brilliance

Making designer jewelry with crystal beads

Anna Elizabeth Draeger

KALMBACH BOOKS

Kalmbach Books
21027 Crossroads Circle
Waukesha, Wisconsin 53186
www.Kalmbach.com/Books

Photography © 2010 Kalmbach Books

Crystal illustrations on p. 4–11 courtesy
of Swarovski. Certain proprietary color
names are trademarked by Swarovski and
are used for informational purposes only.
Crystal products were provided courtesy
of the CREATE YOUR STYLE with
CRYSTALLIZED™ – *Swarovski Elements*
program.

Published in 2010
14 13 12 11 10   1 2 3 4 5

Manufactured in the United States
of America

ISBN: 978-0-87116-295-3

Publisher's Cataloging in Publication Data
Draeger, Anna Elizabeth.
    Crystal brilliance : making designer jewelry
with crystal beads / Anna Elizabeth Draeger.
        p. : ill. (chiefly col.) ; cm.
    ISBN: 978-0-87116-295-3

1. Beadwork–Handbooks, manuals, etc.
2. Beadwork–Patterns. 3. Jewelry making.
I. Title.

TT860 .D73 2010
745.594/2

Contents

Introduction   4

Projects
CLASSIC   12
    Crown Jewels *fringe*   14
    Princess *peyote stitch, chevron chain*   16
    Queen *netting*   18
    Majesty *right-angle weave*   20
    Courtly *modified netting*   23
    Victoria *peyote stitch, fringe*   26
    Promenade *modified netting*   29

ROMANTIC   32
    Lattice *chevron chain*   34
    Antique Lace *chevron chain*   36
    Fairy Dust *right-angle weave, fringe*   39
    Starlight *modified netting*   42
    Belle *peyote stitch, stringing*   44
    Coquette *modified netting, stringing*   48

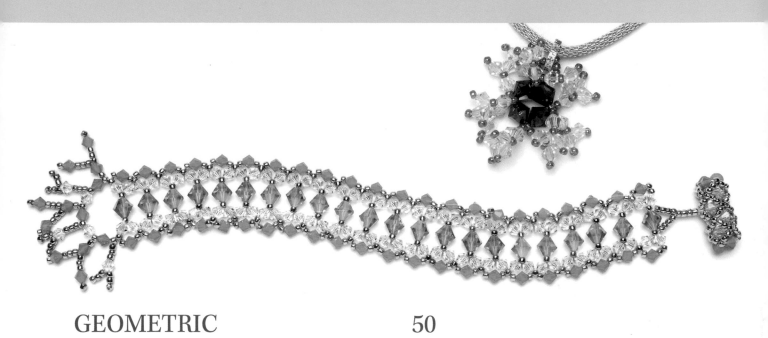

GEOMETRIC 50

Metropolitan *chevron chain*   52

Cubist *right-angle weave*   54

XOXO *netting*   57

Sputnik *right-angle weave, stringing*   60

Bright Lights *netting*   62

Cages *right-angle weave*   65

ORGANIC 68

Clusters *daisy chain, netting*   70

Droplets *peyote stitch*   73

Aurora *peyote stitch*   75

Tide Pool *netting*   78

Featherweight *herringbone, fringe*   80

Lily *modified spiral rope*   83

Curved Branch *herringbone, fringe*   87

BASICS 90

Introduction

The smallest things can change your life.

In 1991, a decision to stop in a hobby store with my best friend did just that. On a whim, we bought some brightly colored seed beads. Stringing those little, inexpensive bits of glass touched something deep inside of me. I felt grounded—instantly connected with the desire to create with my hands.

At first, I spent hours making single-strand necklaces. I strung the beads on thread, which I simply knotted to a clasp. But it wasn't enough. I had already begun to wonder what would happen if I wove the beads together. I grabbed some embroidery floss, split the strands, strung some beads, split the strands again, and strung more beads, creating what looked like peyote stitch.

I had no idea back then that such a thing as peyote stitch existed. I soon found out when I discovered *Bead&Button* magazine. I couldn't believe so many people loved beads

that a magazine was devoted to this hobby. I spent all my free time making bracelets, necklaces, and earrings, and covering just about any object I could find with beads.

I didn't realize then that I was honing the skills that would become my livelihood. Without a teacher, I struggled through each stitch until I mastered it, figuring out how to untangle knots, thread needles in a heartbeat, as well as solve problems as they arose.

A watershed event in my beading adventure occurred the following year while visiting a friend's mom in New York. Claire took us to Woodstock, a town full of delightful shops, which just happened to be the home of a huge supplier called Beyond Beadery. I walked through the door of this bead store and stood in what could only be described as shocked delight. A wall of shimmering crystals in a rainbow of colors took my breath away. I spent every cent I had in that store.

The illustrations along the bottom of p. 4–11 are a guide to the colors and effects in the Crystallized Swarovski Elements product line. These high-quality crystal beads were used to make all the projects in this book.

* Color exclusive to Swarovski

Crystal 001	White Opal 234	White Alabaster* 281	Rose Water Opal* 206	Rose Alabaster* 203	Vintage Rose* 319	Light Rose 223	Rose 209	Rosaline 508	Indian Pink* 289	Fuchsia 502	Ruby 501

I always have been attracted to sparkling things. When I was young, I noticed all the beautiful jewelry my aunties and grandmas wore. I was a collector, picking up anything on the way home from school that caught my eye (even a pretty piece of granite). Now I collect what I think of as the most precious material of all: crystal.

What keeps me entranced with crystals is the ever-changing array. New colors, finishes, and shapes constantly call out to be worked into jewelry designs.

My favorite crystal shape is the bicone. I love fitting the crystals together, and this shape works perfectly for that. The incredible range of colors makes it easy to be inspired.

Many trends come and go, but the way crystals make people feel will always be in fashion. You can mix crystals with many different materials or throw in just a few for a bit of sparkle. I, on the other hand, like to put my crystals front and center.

How to use this book

Many of the projects in this book can be tackled by anyone who's motivated, even a beginner. It may help you to know that each section leads off with a project that I consider fairly easy to do, and each subsequent project gets a little bit more challenging. I often make a component, then repeat it. This really helps to learn the technique, and once the project is done, you'll have a new, useful tool in your repertoire.

You'll find four project sections that group my designs into Classic, Romantic, Geometric, and Organic styles. For those who are unfamiliar with the basic techniques of bead stitching, turn to page 90 for a summary. Whenever a fundamental skill is used in the instructions, you'll see a note to refer to this section.

Padparadscha*	Sun	Fireopal*	Hyacinth	Indian Red*	Light Siam	Dark Red Coral*	Siam	Garnet	Burgundy*
542	248	237	236	374	227	396	208	241	515

Color

Choosing colors for your jewelry projects can be challenging. A good starting point is working with your favorite colors – that's what I do most of time. If you're not sure what your favorites are, look at your wardrobe: What colors do you wear most often? Start with those. If you want to re-create my color choices, you'll appreciate the listing of the exact colors and finishes I used that accompanies each project.

As you'll see in these pages, I love working in greens, blues, and purples—cool colors. Others may prefer warm colors—red, orange, yellow. My colors tend to be analogous; that is, they sit next to each other on the color wheel, creating a quiet harmony in my jewelry. I like a monochromatic color scheme as well, which features different values, or intensities, of the same hue. I love colors that are soothing, one flowing right into the next.

Color is personal. Sometimes I try to work with colors I really dislike, just to push myself out of my comfort zone.

I recall struggling through an entire project I hated, frustrated all the way, only to have my sister tell me how much she loved my color choices!

When I identify a color inspiration, I make a note of it. Later, at the bead store, I pick out crystals to lead off the color group first; it's easier to match seed beads to crystals because seed beads come in an even wider array of colors.

Crystal shapes and sizes

Two of my favorite crystal shapes are the bicone and the round. The bicone is definitely my number-one crystal choice, as it is with most beaders, and most of the designs in this book feature bicones. The bicone is a versatile, economical, and quintessential crystal bead. The Xilion is the patented bicone shape from the Crystallized Swarovski Elements line, and it's even more sparkly than the traditional bicone. It can be used whenever bicones are called for.

I also love to work with Swarovski Elements crystal pearls, which are beautifully perfect imitations of natural pearls. These pearls begin with a spherical crystal core, which is

Light Amethyst	Violet Opal*	Violet	Tanzanite	Amethyst	Purple Velvet*	Dark Indigo*	Montana	Capri Blue	Sapphire	Light Sapphire
212	389	371	055	204	277	288	207	243	206	211

coated in several layers of iridescent material that is similar to the nacre of real pearls. The crystal core gives crystal pearls the weight of real pearls, and they are available in many gorgeous colors. The holes are consistent and larger than those in natural pearls, which makes them easier to incorporate into stitching projects, and the size of every pearl in the strand is consistent.

To supplement the sparkling crystals and the occasional pearl, I usually choose seed beads, bugles, and cylinder beads. I prefer Japanese-made beads because they are consistent in size and shape, and that is the type of seed bead used in the projects. Czech beads, which usually are sold on hanks, give a more uneven texture to beadwork (which sometimes is desirable). Many of my designs require precise, smooth stitches, and using consistent beads will lead to even stitches.

Culling beads

Choose your beads carefully, and don't hesitate to discard any misshapen beads or crystals with rough edges. This is called culling. If a seed bead is lopsided, discard it. If a bugle bead has

a broken edge or is shorter than the others, discard it. Always use the best quality to create the finest jewelry.

Findings

I prefer sterling silver or gold-filled findings. Using precious metals like these will help avoid any skin irritation due to allergies. Base, or low-quality, metals cause reactions for some people, and this becomes a special consideration if you give your creations as gifts. Solid silver or gold-filled findings also ensure that your jewelry will last; if you use plated findings, you may find that the finish wears off over time.

To attach clasps to the ends of beading wire, I prefer crimp tubes to crimp beads for a professional look. Again, I use precious metals—sterling silver and gold-filled crimps, which are easier to crimp and hold up better than base metal crimps. I also like to use 3 mm crimp covers for a finishing touch in my jewelry.

Aquamarine
202

Air Blue Opal*
285

Light Azore*
361

Indian Sapphire*
217

Pacific Opal*
390

Mint Alabaster*
397

Turquoise
267

Indicolite
379

Caribbean Blue Opal*
394

Blue Zircon
229

Needles

Long beading needles are my favorite; I suggest you keep numbers 10, 12, and 13 in your stash. Of these, #10s are the biggest, and they are the easiest to thread. If you find they are too big to fit through certain beads, you can always switch to a thinner needle.

Beading thread

Fireline is my first choice when stitching with beads and crystals. This single-ply polyethylene fiber stands up very well to the sharp edges of crystals and bugles. It has no stretch, so your beadwork will not loosen with wear. Most often I use 6 lb. test; a common range for beading is 4–8 lb. test.

All the projects in the book call for Fireline, but you may choose to substitute your favorite beading thread. I usually use the dark neutral color called Smoke; it works well with most medium- to dark-colored beads. Smoke Fireline has a residue that can be wiped off with a damp cloth before working with it, or you can run it through Thread Heaven or beeswax to keep the residue from coming off on your hands as you work. It isn't a big deal, though—it washes right off.

The other color option in Fireline is Crystal; it is white and works well with lighter crystals and beads.

Keep your working length of thread manageable—I suggest just an arm's length or two. If you try to use a longer thread, it will most likely tangle up and frustrate you. I usually work with a single thread. Keep the needle near the end of your working thread. The point where the eye of the needle sits will be a weak spot in the thread and can compromise your beadwork. Also, the more thread you pull through the needle, the more likely it is that tangling and knotting will occur.

Beginning and ending thread

Since you'll be working with fairly short lengths of thread, you may need to start a new thread before you complete a bracelet project, and most certainly as you're stitching a necklace. You don't want to lose beads or see all of your hard work start to come undone. It's easy to avoid this by adding new thread and ending thread properly. When I'm down to about 6–8 in. (15–20 cm) of thread, I weave back through the beadwork that I just finished, crossing the thread over itself if possible, following the same thread path and tying a few half-hitch

Chrysolite	Peridot	Erinite	Emerald	Palace Green Opal	Olivine	Khaki	Lime	Silk	Light Topaz	Jonquil	Jet
238	214	360	205	393	228	550	385	249	226	213	391

knots as I go. The weaving is definitely more important than the knots; it locks the thread in place and makes a secure end.

Take time to end your project properly, because rushing this step will waste all the time you spend creating if your work ends up falling apart. My favorite solution is to incorporate a beaded clasp as a finishing touch. If I opt to use a purchased clasp, I don't sew it directly to the project; instead, I make a loop of seed beads, and use jump rings to connect the two.

Thread tension

I often joke that my beadwork is so tight because I'm so stressed out. It's true! Sometimes my tension is so tight that I can't fit the thinnest needle through on a second thread pass. Do as I say, not as I do: Try to maintain even, moderately tight tension as you work. (I'm working on it!)

The way you hold your work will affect your tension. After I pull a stitch through, I hold the thread with my thumb and index finger where the thread exits the last bead. I keep holding that until the next stitch is worked and I've pulled the new

thread through. This way, the previous stitch can't loosen before the next is completed. You can always go back and retrace a thread path if you can't seem to get the right tension the first time around. It's much easier to pull everything tight when the beads are already in place.

The most important thing you're trying to achieve with the right tension is to minimize the amount of thread showing. Some stitches like herringbone are more prone to having the thread show, and that's OK—it's just the nature of the stitch.

Stretching and stengthening

Having lived with painful tendinitis for the past few years, I cannot stress how important it is to take care of your hands. Do this by taking frequent breaks and using ergonomic tools. Stand up, walk around, and stretch at intervals. Try to maintain good posture while you work as well.

I've been a hard-core beader for twenty years. I spent a lot of that time hunched over my bead tray for hours on end. When I started working at

 Light Peach*
362

 Light Colorado Topaz
246

 Topaz
203

 Light Smoked Topaz*
221

 Smoked Topaz
220

 Mocca*
286

 Smoky Quartz*
225

Sand Opal*
287

Light Grey Opal*
383

 Black Diamond
215

 Jet
280

the magazine, where I'm either at my computer or beading at my desk, I had to stop beading so much at home because I simply couldn't do it anymore. I try to remember to take my doctor's advice to pause and stretch.

I've worked on undoing the damage hunching over has done by working on my back muscles, strengthening the core muscles that help me sit up straight as I work. As for my hands—I protect them at all costs. I rest when I feel pain, and I stretch my fingers every so often when I'm beading.

As long as you haven't yet developed any problems, you can practice preventative stretching (check with your doctor first if you have questions).

Work area
A soft work surface will help you have pleasant and productive beading sessions. You want a surface large enough to spread out all your beads and beadwork if necessary. I use a large piece of Vellux on my beading table. If I'm watching TV while working, I use a portable lap desk.

Keep the area around you clear of anything that can snag your working thread. There's nothing more annoying than catching your tools or other items in your thread and getting a big, tangled mess. That goes for jewelry as well; a large beaded bracelet is just asking to be a menace.

Make sure you have proper lighting. It will help you work for longer stretches and you'll save your eyes from a lot of strain. Without proper lighting, little things like a thread catching around a bead can easily slip past your notice. I use a floor lamp with a full-spectrum bulb positioned directly over my work tray, and I flood the room with as much light as possible. Natural light is always my first choice. I love working in sunlight, and my favorite place is on my backyard patio. I can watch my kids play as I bead (as long as the Wisconsin weather cooperates).

Creating new designs
Inspiration can strike anywhere at any time. Be aware of this and allow yourself to be open to it. Prepare for it by carrying a sketch pad or a camera wherever you go, so when you see something that catches your attention, you're ready. I'm often

Effects *Some effects are special production only*

Crystal Aurore Boreale	Crystal Aurore Boreale 2	Crystal Satin*	Crystal Matt Finish	Crystal Moonlight*	Crystal Silver Shade*	Crystal Golden Shadow*	Crystal Copper*	Crystal Red Magma*	Crystal Comet Argent Light
001 AB	001 AB2	001 SAT	001 MAT	001 MOL	001 SSHA	001 GSHA	001 COP	001 REDM	001 CAL

struck by a color combination or delicate geometric shapes, and when I see something that gets my creative gears turning, I make a small sketch, noting the basic shape, what colors I think would look good, the sizes of crystals and beads I would use, and what I think the end project would be.

When I first started working on projects from magazines or books, I'd copy them exactly to learn the techniques. As my skills grew, I realized that I wanted to teach others, and I knew I'd have to come up with projects of my own design.

My favorite way to come up with new design ideas is to simply play with my beads. I spread them out around me and pick through the shapes and colors, organizing them in some way. Then I get started. Most of the time when I'm beading, a project will begin to emerge, and as it does, I take careful note of how the beads are sitting together. If there is too much of a gap between the beads, or if I think a different bead would work better in the stitch, I'll keep it in mind. I usually redo a project four or five times to make sure every bead sits perfectly.

A good way to begin designing is to learn each stitch and practice until you really master it. Observe how a project comes together, and think about how you might have done it differently. Challenge yourself to make something without looking at anyone else's design. Or look in a fashion magazine and find a piece of fine jewelry you really like and try to mimic it in beads. You may be surprised at what you can come up with this way.

If you really enjoy making other people's designs, such as those in this book, then do that. Just remember to be ethical and fair: Don't sell, copy, or teach someone else's designs without their permission. Whichever beading path you choose, the most important thing is to just keep working and enjoying the process.

White Opal Sky Blue*
234 SBL

White Opal Star Shine*
234 STS

Crystal Bermuda Blue
001 BBL

Crystal Heliotrope
001 HEL

Crystal Metallic Blue 2x*
001 METBL2

Crystal Vitrail Medium
001 VM

Crystal Dorado 2x*
001 DOR2

Jet Nut 2x*
280 NUT2

Jet Hematite
280 HEM

Jet Hematite 2x
280 HEM2

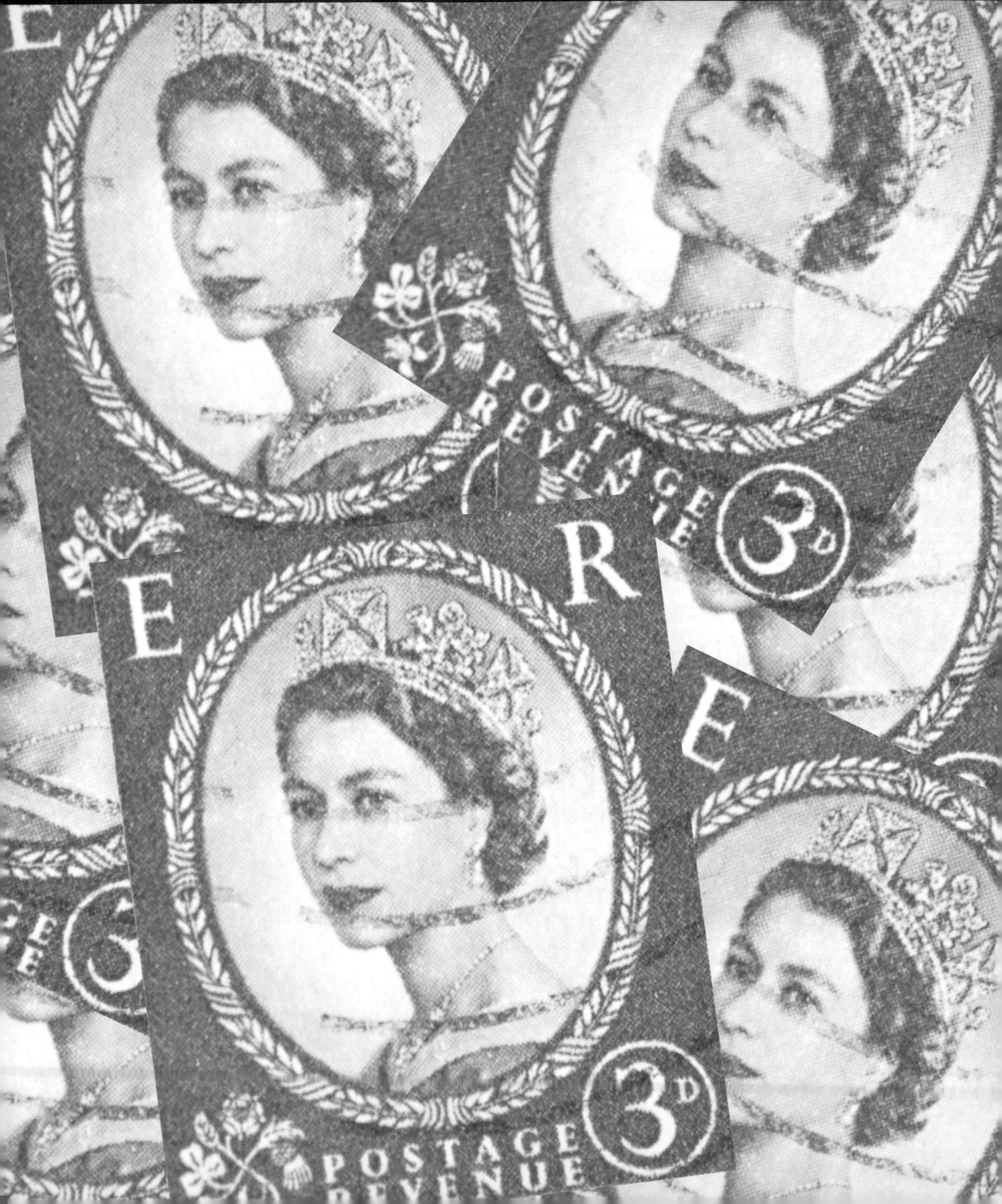
E
R
POSTAGE
REVENUE
3D

CLASSIC

These timeless and elegant designs will always be in style.

Crown Jewels

This bracelet has all the appeal of the classic tennis bracelet. Don't you love knowing that you can stitch one up in just one sitting?

MATERIALS

For a 7½-in. (19.1 cm) bracelet
- 4 mm bicone crystals
  22 color A
  65 color B
- 2 g 15º seed beads
- Clasp
- 2 jump rings
- Fireline 6 lb. test
- Beading needles, #12
- 2 pairs of pliers

1 Attach a stop bead (Basics) to 2 yd. (1.8 m) of Fireline, leaving a 10-in. (25 cm) tail.

2 Pick up a color A 4 mm, a B 4 mm, and a 15º seed bead. Skip the 15º, and sew back through the B **[fig. 1]**.

3 Pick up two Bs and a 15º. Skip the 15º, and sew back through the last B **[fig. 2]**.

4 Pick up an A, a B, and a 15º. Skip the 15º, and sew back through the B **[fig. 3]**.

Featured bracelet
4 mm bicone crystals:
  Chrysolite (color A),
  Jet AB 2X (color B)
15º seed beads: gold-lined
  rainbow aqua

Solid green bracelet
4 mm bicone crystals: Jet AB 2X
15º seed beads: gold-lined
  rainbow aqua

Design option
4 mm bicone crystals: Crystal
  Bermuda (color A), Montana
  (color B)
15º seed beads, gunmetal

Tip Your bracelet will probably twist as you work. Zigzagging back through the center row of crystals helps it to lie flat. Once the bracelet is clasped on your arm, it will lie straight.

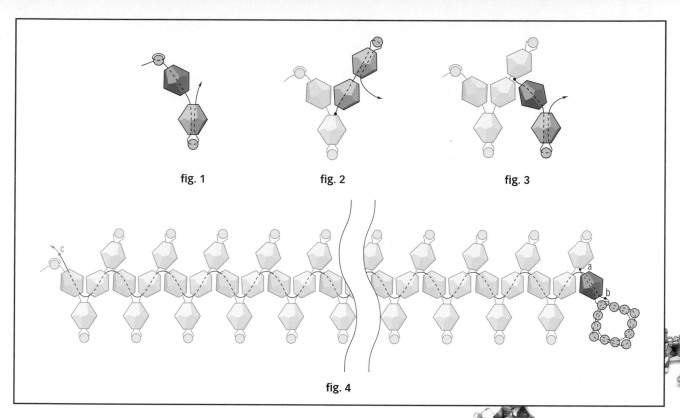

fig. 1

fig. 2

fig. 3

fig. 4

5 Repeat steps 3 and 4 until you reach the desired length, ending with step 3. Keep in mind that the clasp will add about an inch to the finished length.

6 Pick up an A and twelve 15ºs. Sew through the 15ºs again, skipping every third 15º to bring the beads into a square shape [**fig. 4, a–b**]. Reinforce the bracelet

by sewing back through the center crystals [**b–c**]. End the thread (Basics).

7 Remove the stop bead on the beginning end of the bracelet, and repeat step 6.

8 Open a jump ring (Basics), attach half of the clasp to one end of the bracelet, and close the jump ring. Repeat on the other end.

Tip Crystals with multiple coatings, like Jet AB 2X, really light up your wrist; try subtle colors for everyday wear.

Design Option

If you give your jewelry as a gift, offering length options is always a plus. Here's one idea: Simply incorporate a multiple-loop toggle clasp like this one for easy adjustment.

Princess

Kick your stitching up a notch by incorporating a beaded clasp.

MATERIALS

For a 7¾-in. (19.7 cm) bracelet

- 4 mm bicone crystals:
  54 color A
  51 color B
- 2 g 11º cylinder beads
- 4 g 15º seed beads
- ½ in. (1.3 cm) small-link chain
- Fireline 6 lb. test
- Beading needles, #13
- Wire cutters

Toggle loop

1 On 1 yd. (.9 m) of Fireline, alternate one 15º and one 11º cylinder until you have 24 beads. Sew through the first two beads again **[fig. 1, a–b]**, leaving a 12-in. (30 cm) tail.

2 Working in tubular peyote stitch **(Basics)**, pick up a cylinder, and sew through the next cylinder in the ring **[b–c]**. Repeat around the ring, and step up through the first cylinder added in the round **[c–d]**.

3 Work one more round with cylinders **[d–e]**. Work the last round with 15ºs **[e–f]**, pulling tight so it forms a tire-shaped ring. Reinforce all the rounds.

4 End the working thread (Basics), but leave the tail.

Toggle bar

1 On 1 yd. (.9 m) of Fireline, leave a 6-in. (15 cm) tail, and pick up 11 cylinders **[fig. 2, a–b]**. Skip the last two cylinders, and sew through the third cylinder from the needle, sewing towards the tail **[b–c]**. Working in even-count peyote (Basics), pick up a cylinder, skip a cylinder, and sew through the next cylinder **[c–d]**. Repeat to complete the row **[d–e]**. Continue in peyote for nine rows to make a strip six cylinders wide and ten cylinders long **[e–f]**.

2 Roll the strip into a tube, and zip up the end beads (Basics). End the tail but leave the working thread.

3 Sew through the beadwork to exit a cylinder in the center of the peyote tube. Sew through the end link on the chain, and sew through an adjacent cylinder in the tube. Retrace the thread path a few times to secure the connection, and end the thread.

Bracelet band

1 On 2 yd. (1.8 m) of Fireline, leaving an 8-in. (20 cm) tail, pick up a cylinder, a color A 4 mm, two cylinders, an A, two cylinders, and a color B 4 mm. Sew back through the first cylinder [fig. 3, a–b].

2 Pick up a cylinder, an A, two cylinders, and a B. Sew back through the last cylinder added in the previous stitch [b–c].

3 Repeat step 2 until you reach the desired length [c–d]. Work one more stitch, but use only A 4 mms [d-e].

4 Using the tail from the toggle loop, sew into the end stitch of the bracelet band, entering at the *. Retrace the thread path several times, and end the thread.

5 Using the working thread from the bracelet, sew to the * at the other end, and sew through the end link on the chain to connect the toggle bar. Retrace the thread path several times, and end the thread.

COLORS

Featured bracelet

4 mm bicone crystals: Purple Velvet (color A), Montana AB 2X (color B)
11º cylinder beads: metallic purple iris
15º seed beads: purple iris

Design option—purple

3 mm bicone crystals: Purple Velvet
11º cylinder beads: silver-lined dark purple
15º seed beads: purple iris

Design option—green

3 mm bicone crystals: Pacific Opal AB
11º cylinder beads: matte metallic dark green iris
15º seed beads: green iris

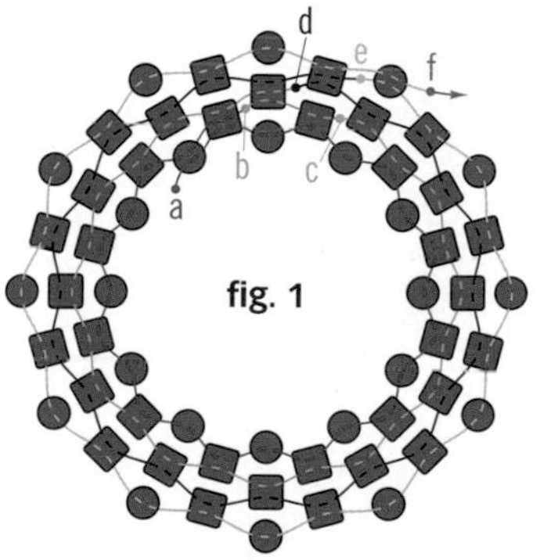

fig. 1

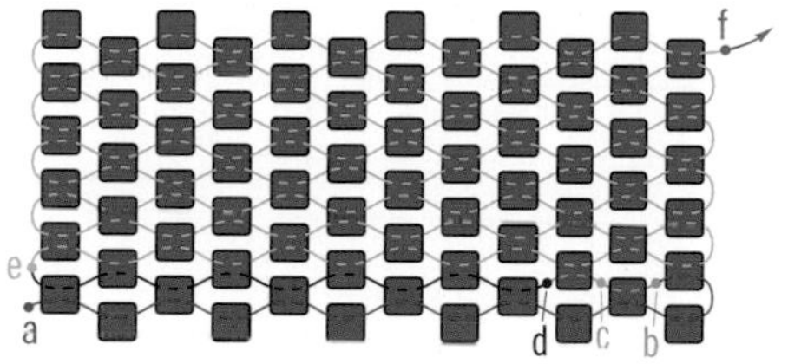

fig. 2

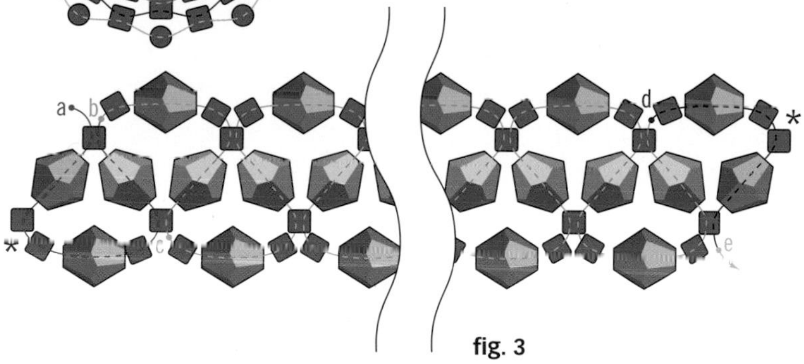

fig. 3

Tip If you have trouble keeping the shape of the peyote ring as you're stitching, try forming it around a small dowel or a pencil.

Design Option

Make just the clasp to use with any project, and spruce it up with 3 mm crystals circling the center round of peyote.

Queen

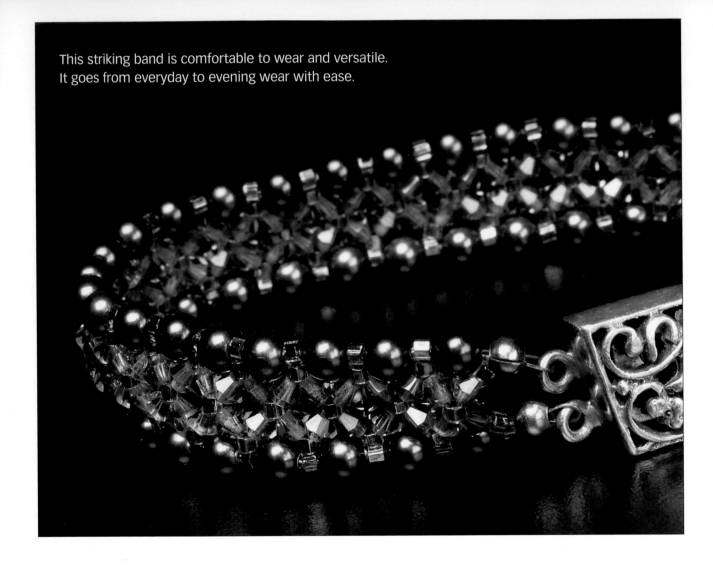

This striking band is comfortable to wear and versatile. It goes from everyday to evening wear with ease.

MATERIALS

For a 7-in. (18 cm) bracelet

- 60 4 mm round pearls
- 120 3 mm bicone crystals
- 3 g 11º cylinder beads
- 2-strand clasp
- 4 crimp beads
- Fireline 6 lb. test
- Flexible beading wire, .012
- Beading needles, #12
- Tape or 2 Bead Stoppers
- Crimping pliers
- Wire cutters

Tip Use a Bead Stopper or a small piece of tape to secure the end of the beading wire.

1 Cut two 12-in. (30 cm) pieces of flexible beading wire. On one wire, string a crimp bead and one loop of a 2-strand clasp. Go back through the crimp bead, and crimp it (Basics). Repeat with the other wire and the other clasp loop. On one wire, string a pattern of a cylinder and a 4 mm round pearl **[fig. 1]** 30 times, ending with a cylinder. Temporarily secure the end of the wire with tape or a Bead Stopper. Repeat with the second wire.

Note: As you begin stitching, sew through only pearls on the first wire and only cylinders on the second wire.

2 Thread a needle on 2 yd. (1.8 m) of Fireline, and sew through the first cylinder on one of the wires. Pick up a cylinder, a 3 mm, a cylinder, a 3 mm and a cylinder, and sew through the first cylinder on the other wire **[fig. 2, a–b]**. Sew back through the last five beads picked up, and continue through the first cylinder, 4 mm, and the next cylinder **[b–c]**.

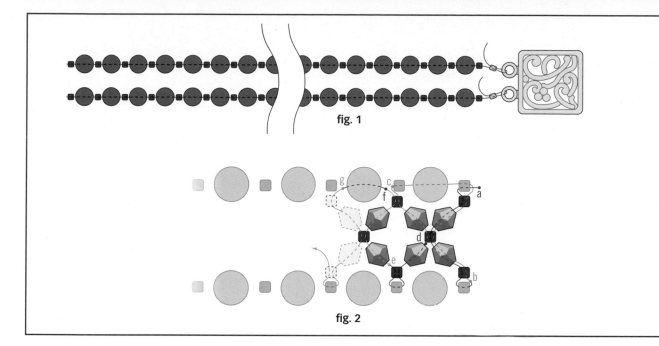

fig. 1

fig. 2

3 Pick up a cylinder and a 3 mm, and sew through the center cylinder from the previous step **[c–d]**. Pick up a 3 mm and a cylinder, and sew through the next cylinder on the second wire. Sew back through the last cylinder picked up **[d–e]**.

4 Pick up a 3 mm, a cylinder, and a 3 mm, and sew back through the first cylinder picked up in the previous step **[e–f]**. Then sew through the next pearl on the wire **[f–g]**.

5 Repeat steps 3 and 4 until you reach the other end of the bracelet.

6 End the working thread and tail (Basics).

7 Remove the tape or Bead Stopper from one wire, and string a crimp bead and a loop of the other half of the clasp. Go back through the crimp bead, crimp it, and trim the excess wire. Repeat with the other wire and remaining clasp loop.

COLORS

Featured bracelet
4 mm round pearls: dark green
3 mm bicone crystals: Black Diamond Champagne
11º cylinder beads: lined topaz AB hex cut

Design option
5 mm pearls: dark green
4 mm bicone crystals: Tourmaline Satin
11º seed beads: gold luster fern

Tip Maintain even tension along the crystal netting by making sure the thread isn't showing on the previous stitch before you move on to the next stitch.

Design Option

Use bigger beads: Substitute 5 or 6 mm bicone crystals for the pearls, 4 mm bicones for the 3 mms, and 11º seed beads for the 11º cylinders.

Majesty

Using the same technique with different sizes of crystals produces beaded beads for a necklace that sparkles like crazy. These right-angle-weave beads are versatile—use them in necklaces, bracelets, and earrings.

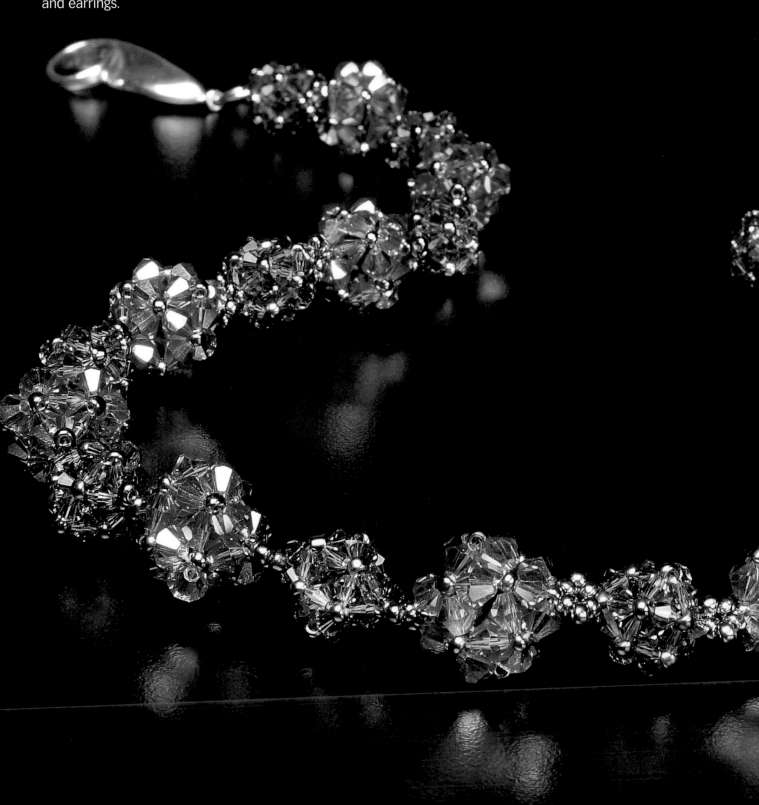

MATERIALS

For an 18-in. (46 cm) necklace

- 288 4 mm bicone crystals
- 312 3 mm bicone crystals
- 5 g 11º seed beads
- Clasp
- 2 jump rings
- Fireline 6 lb. test
- Beading needles, #12
- 2 pairs of pliers

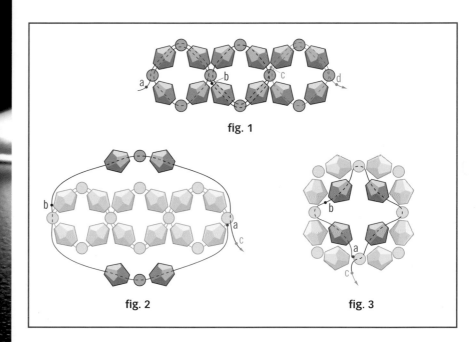

fig. 1

fig. 2　　　　fig. 3

1 On a comfortable length of Fireline, pick up a repeating pattern of an 11º and a 3 mm four times, leaving a 6-in. (15 cm) tail. Sew through the first five beads again to exit the 11º opposite the tail **[fig. 1, a–b]**.

2 Pick up a repeating pattern of a 3 mm and an 11º three times, and pick up a 3 mm. Sew through the 11º your thread exited at the start of this step and the next four beads **[b–c]**. Repeat **[c–d]**.

3 To form the strip into a ring, pick up a 3 mm, an 11º, and a 3 mm. Sew through the 11º at the opposite end of the beadwork **[fig. 2, a–b]**. Repeat **[b–c]** and sew through the next 3 mm and 11º along one edge.

4 Pick up a 3 mm, and sew through the next edge 11º **[fig. 3, a–b]**. Repeat three times **[b–c]**, pulling the beads snug.

Tip If you can't get your tension tight enough, try sewing through each stitch with a second thread path.

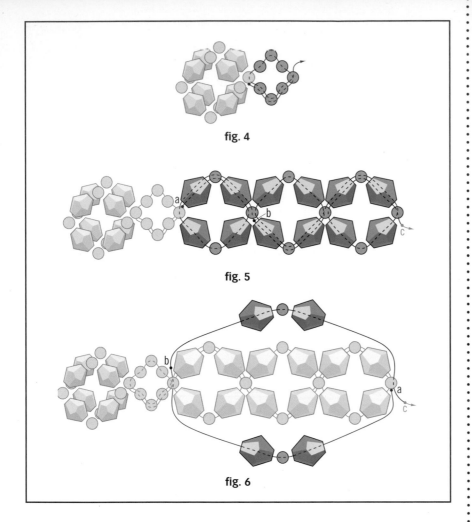

fig. 4

fig. 5

fig. 6

Design Option

Make two extra beaded beads for gorgeous drop earrings. You'll need earring findings and two soldered jump rings.

5 Sew through the beadwork to exit an 11º on the other edge, and repeat step 4.

6 Pick up seven 11ºs, and sew through the 11º your thread exited at the start of this step. Sew through the next four 11ºs **[fig. 4]**

7 Pick up a pattern of a 4 mm and an 11º three times, and pick up a 4 mm. Sew through the 11º your thread exited at the start of this step and the next four beads **[fig. 5, a–b]**. Repeat twice **[b–c]**.

8 Pick up a 4 mm, an 11º, and a 4 mm. Sew through the opposite 11º **[fig. 6, a–b]**. Repeat **[b–c]**.

9 Sew through the next 11º and 4 mm along one edge. Add 4 mms to the open edges as in steps 4 and 5.

10 Pick up seven 11ºs, and sew through the 11º your thread exited at the start of this step. Sew through the next four 11ºs.

11 Continue making small and large beads as in steps 1–10 until you have 13 3 mm beads and 12 4 mm beads, ending and adding thread (Basics) as needed.

12 Repeat step 6 on both ends of the necklace, and end the thread.

13 Open a jump ring (Basics) and attach half a clasp to an end loop. Close the jump ring. Repeat on the other end.

1 Work steps 1–5 to make a beaded bead, and exit an 11º.

2 Pick up 20 11ºs and a soldered jump ring. Sew back through the 20 11ºs and into the 11º in the beaded bead. End the thread (Basics).

3 Open the loop on an earring finding (Basics), attach it to the jump ring, and close the jump ring.

4 Repeat steps 1–3 to make a second earring.

Rows of bicones nestle together in a linear pattern that highlights the larger crystal beads. Finish off this beauty with a custom clasp that blends right in.

Victoria

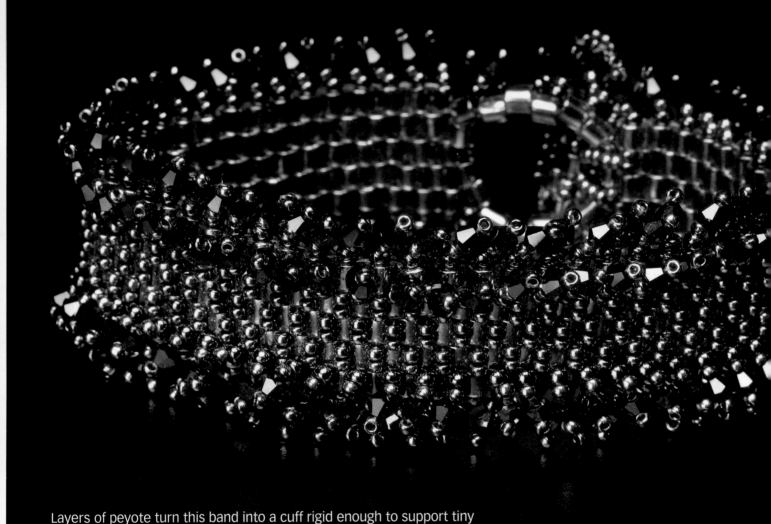

Layers of peyote turn this band into a cuff rigid enough to support tiny rows of crystal fringes. Be advised: This bracelet commands attention!

MATERIALS

For a 7½-in. (19.1 cm) bracelet

- 225–250 3 mm bicone crystals
- 12 g 8º cylinder beads
- 5 g 11º seed beads
- 10 g 15º seed beads
- Fireline 6 lb. test
- Beading needles, #12

Toggle bar

1 On 2 yd. (1.8 m) of Fireline, leave a 6-in. (15 cm) tail, and make an odd-count peyote strip (Basics) five beads wide and ten rows long using 8º cylinder beads [**fig. 1**]. Roll the strip into a tube, zip up the ends (Basics), and sew back to the other end.

2 With the thread exiting an end 8º of the tube, pick up an 11º, a 15º, a 3 mm crystal, and a 15º. Skip the 15º, and sew back through the 3 mm, the 15º, the 11º, and the end 8º [**fig. 2**]. Pick up two 15ºs, and sew

through the next 8º in the same row [**fig. 3**]. Repeat once, exiting the end 8º in the same row. Make a fringe on this end, and then sew back to the other end, adding two 15ºs between the two 8ºs in the next row [**fig. 4**]. Continue adding fringe along both ends of the bead and two 15ºs between each peyote stitch in each row.

3 After you've added all five fringes on each end, sew through the nearest fringe to exit the end 15º. Sew through the 15ºs at the end of the fringe to pull them into a ring

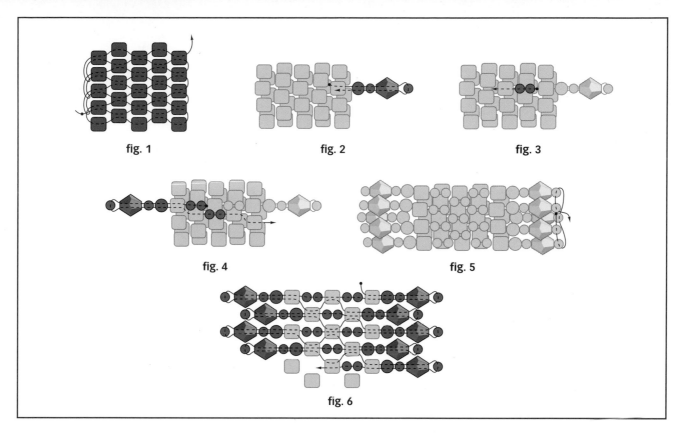

fig. 1

fig. 2

fig. 3

fig. 4

fig. 5

fig. 6

[fig. 5]. Sew through to the other end, and repeat. End the threads (Basics).

4 On a new 3-yd. (2.7 m) length of Fireline, make an odd-count band as in step 1, but continue until the band is about 1 in. (2.5 cm) short of your desired length, ending with three beads on one end and two on the other.

5 On a new 3-yd. (2.7 m) length of Fireline, leave an 18-in. (46 cm) tail, and embellish the base in the same manner as the toggle, but add a second row of fringe along the second-to-last end row of 8ºs. Embellish one row, then sew back to the starting side, then embellish the next row, and sew back to the starting side [**fig. 6**]. **Note:** Beads in the figure are spread to show the thread path.

Tip Pull the 3 mm bicone and the 15º seed bead up to the base before sewing back through the 3 mm. Hold the 3 mm in place so the 15º doesn't stop you from getting the 3 mm as close to the base as possible.

Featured bracelet
3 mm bicone crystals: Garnet
8º cylinders: amber-lined
    topaz AB
15º seed beads: bronze

Design option—silver
3 mm bicone crystals: Crystal
8º cylinder beads: nickel plated
15º seed beads: nickel plated

Design option—blue-gray
3 mm bicone crystals: Indian Sapphire
8º cylinders: transparent gray
    gold luster
15º seed beads: metallic amethyst
    gunmetal

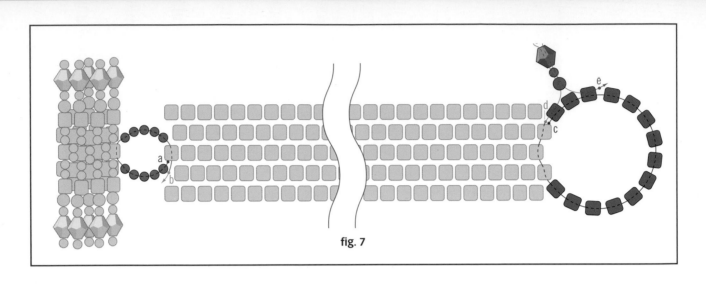

fig. 7

6 Use the tail to sew through two 15ºs and the center 8º on one end of the base. Pick up five 15ºs, sew through a center 8º on the toggle, and pick up five more 15ºs. Sew through the same 8º in the base again, retrace the thread path a few times to reinforce the join, and end tails **[fig. 7, a–b]**.

7 Start a new thread or use what's left from embellishing the base to exit the second 8º on the other end of the bracelet. Pick up enough 8ºs to accommodate the toggle bar, making sure it is an even number, and sew through the three center 8ºs on the edge **[c–d]**. Sew through the next 8º in the loop, and add short fringe as desired **[d–e]**.

Repeat around the loop, and keep checking that the toggle fits through the loop as you embellish, since many thread paths may tighten the loop, preventing the toggle from passing through. End the tails. **Note:** The embellishment is left out of this figure to focus on the toggle and loop.

Design Options

Make a continuous band into a cuff-style bracelet: Stitch a band long enough to fit around the largest part of your hand, zip the ends together (Basics), and embellish. Or try an alternate color palette, like the cool blues and grays in the bracelet below.

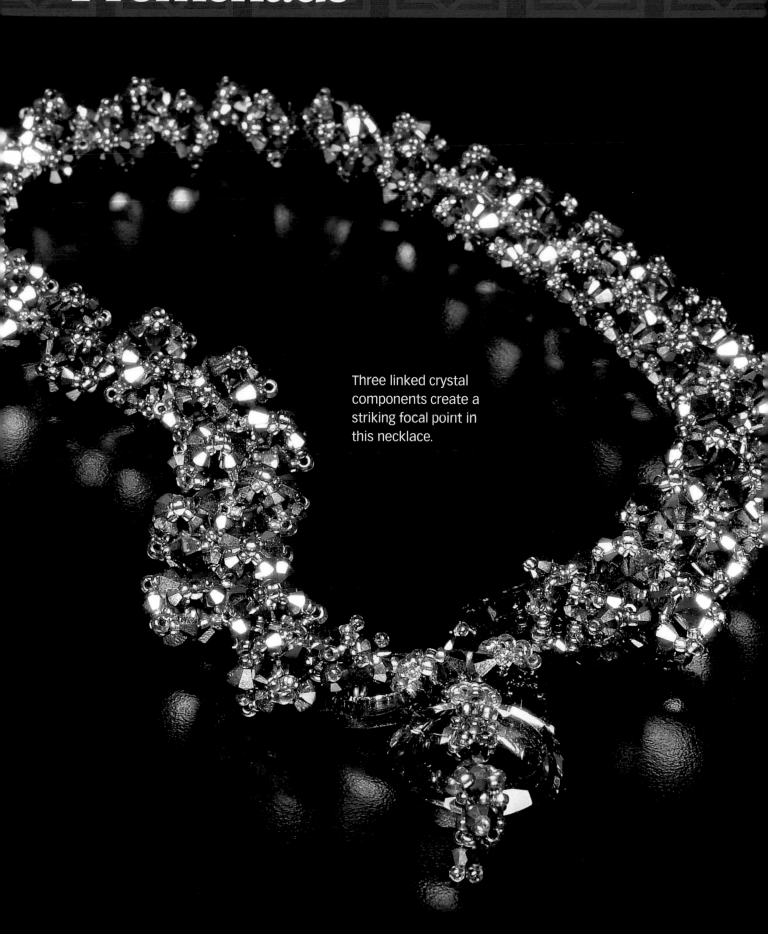

Promenade

Three linked crystal
components create a
striking focal point in
this necklace.

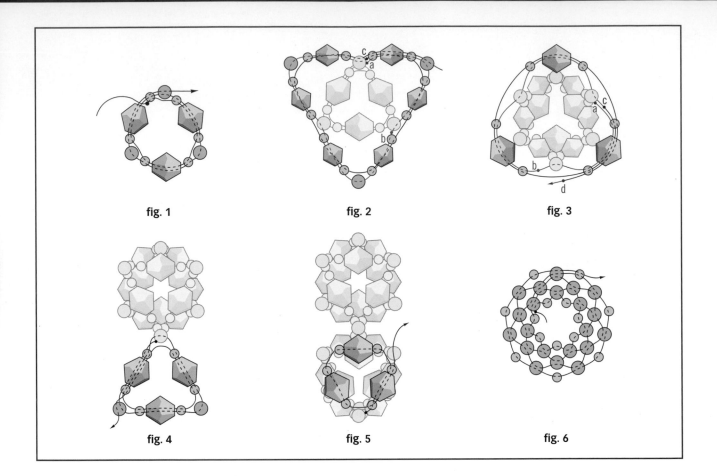

fig. 1

fig. 2

fig. 3

fig. 4

fig. 5

fig. 6

MATERIALS

For a 16-in. (41 cm) necklace

- Crystallized Swarovski Elements
  20 or 30 mm fancy stone #4139
  20 or 30 mm fancy stone #4439
  14 mm fancy stone #4139
- 325 4 mm bicone crystals
- 325 3 mm bicone crystals
- 10 g 11º seed beads
- 20 g 15º seed beads
- Fireline 4 or 6 lb. test
- Beading needles, #12 or 13
- Clasp

Tip Don't stitch too tightly when making your beaded beads, or you'll have a hard time sewing back through to attach the next bead.

1 On a comfortable length of Fireline, pick up a pattern of a 15º, an 11º, a 15º, and a 4 mm three times. Leaving a 12-in. (30 cm) tail, sew through the beads again, but skip the 11ºs. Pull the beads into a tight triangle shape. Step up through the first 15º and 11º **[fig. 1]**.

2 Pick up a 15º, a 3 mm, a 15º, an 11º, a 15º, a 3 mm, and a 15º. Skip the next 15º, 4 mm, and 15º in the previous round, and sew through the next 11º **[fig. 2, a–b]**. Repeat twice **[b–c]**. Sew through all the beads added in this round, but skip the 11ºs, pulling tight so each section forms tight Vs. you may need to use your needle to pop the 11ºs outward. Exit an 11º **[c–d]**.

3 Pick up a 15º, a 4 mm, and a 15º. Sew through the next 11º in the previous round **[fig. 2, a–b]**. Repeat twice **[b–c]**. Sew through the beads in the new round, skipping the 11ºs, to bring the new round

into a tight triangle shape. Exit an 11º **[c–d]**.

4 Pick up a 15º, a 4 mm, a 15º, an 11º, a 15º, a 4 mm, a 15º, an 11º, a 15º, a 4 mm, and a 15º. Sew through the 11º your thread exited and the new beads, skipping the 11ºs as in step 1. Exit an 11º **[fig. 4]**.

5 Repeat steps 2 and 3 to complete the beaded bead. Exit an 11º in the new round that will offset the next beaded bead **[fig. 5]**.

6 Repeat steps 4 and 5 until you reach half the desired length of your necklace strap. Make a second strap. Save the tails on both ends of the necklace straps to connect them to the centerpiece and clasp on both ends.

7 On a new 1-yd. (.9 m) length of Fireline, pick up an even number of 11ºs to fit loosely around the small crystal circle component (rounds 1 and 2; see **fig. 6** for the entire thread path for this step). Sew through the first 11º again to form a ring. Work a round of peyote (Basics) by picking up an 11º, skipping an 11º on the ring, and sewing through the next 11º. Repeat around the ring (round 3), then step up through an 11º in the new round. Work a round of 15ºs along each edge of the 11ºs (rounds 4 and 5), using the working thread for round 4 and the tail for round 5. End the threads. Work a peyote ring around the large circle and square crystal components, saving one working thread to connect the three crystal components together.

8 Arrange the crystal components so the small circle and square are next to each other, the large circle is directly below them, and the peyote rings come together in the center. Line up three 11ºs in the peyote rings, and stitch the three 11ºs together as needed to make a secure connection. To embellish the join, pick up a crystal and a 15º. Sew back through the crystal and the 11º your thread exited. Repeat twice to cover the join with three short fringes.

9 Make a ring of peyote around the large circle, and embellish it with short fringe.

10 Using the tail from one necklace strap, connect the necklace to the small circle with another ring of 15ºs. Embellish the connection if desired.

11 Connect the other strap of the necklace to the square component with another ring of 15ºs, and embellish it.

12 Connect half of the clasp to each necklace strap with a ring of 15ºs. Secure the tails in the beadwork and trim.

Design Option

Make a cool cuff bracelet in the same way.

1 Stitch and connect three beaded beads as in steps 1–5, but make them in a straight line instead of offsetting the third bead. When the zigzagging band of beaded beads is long enough to fit around the widest part of your wrist, stitch the ends together.

2 Continue making beaded beads in a zigzag pattern, connecting three beaded beads in a straight line, then offsetting the next one to begin a new row of beaded beads.

3 String accent rounds of beads through the zigzag rows, stitching through corresponding beads in the beaded beads.

ROMANTIC

Jewelry can evoke a time, a place, or a feeling. These projects
show the soft side of crystals—fancy and feminine.

Lattice

This necklace, with its delicate drape, makes a lovely companion to the following project, the Antique Lace bracelet.

MATERIALS

For an 18-in. (46 cm) necklace

- 22 5 or 6 mm bicone crystals
- 4 mm bicone crystals:
  166 color A
  69 color B
- 60 4 mm crystal pearls
- 5 g 15º seed beads
- Clasp
- Fireline 6 lb. test
- Beading needles, #12

Tip When choosing colors, make sure the darker 4 mm bicone sits along the top of the necklace.

COLORS

4 mm bicone crystals: Ceylon
  Topaz (color A)
5 or 6 mm bicone crystals:
  Mocca (color B)
4 mm pearl: deep brown
15º seed beads: brown iris

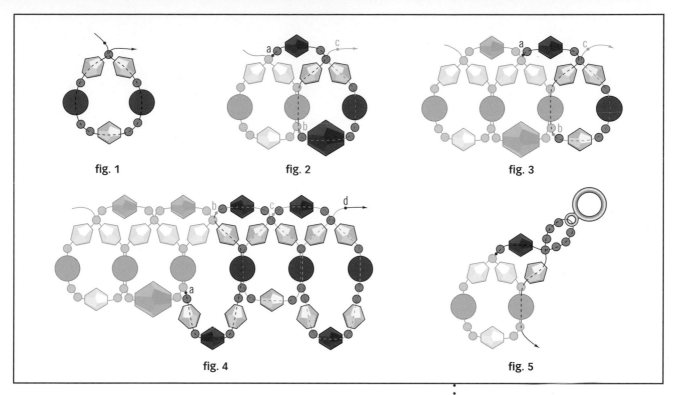

fig. 1

fig. 2

fig. 3

fig. 4

fig. 5

1 On 3 yd. (2.7 m) of Fireline, attach a stop bead (Basics), leaving a 10-in. (25 cm) tail. Pick up a 15º, a color A 4 mm bicone crystal, a 15º, a 4 mm pearl, two 15ºs, an A, two 15ºs, a pearl, a 15º, and an A. Sew back through the first 15º to create a loop **[fig. 1]**.

2 Pick up a 15º, a color B 4 mm bicone crystal, two 15ºs, and an A. Sew through the side 15º, pearl, and 15º in the previous loop **[fig. 2, a–b]**.

3 Pick up a 15º, a 6 mm bicone crystal, two 15ºs, a pearl, a 15º, and an A. Sew through the 15º above the A in the previous step **[b–c]**.

4 Pick up a 15º, a B, two 15ºs, and an A. Sew through the side 15º, pearl, and 15º in the previous loop **[fig. 3, a–b]**.

5 Pick up a 15º, an A, two 15ºs, a pearl, a 15º, and an A. Sew through the 15º above the A in the previous step **[b–c]**.

6 Repeat steps 2 5 until you have 11 6 mm loops. After finishing the last 6 mm loop, work step 2.

7 Pick up a 15º, an A, a 15º, a B, a 15º, an A, two 15ºs, a pcarl, a 15º, and an A. Sew through the 15º above the A in the previous step **[fig. 4, a–b]**.

8 Repeat steps 4 and 5 **[b–c]**, then 4 and 7 **[c–d]** to make a total of nine big loops with eight A loops in between them.

9 Repeat steps 2–5 until you have 11 6 mm loops. End with an A loop.

10 To attach a clasp, pick up a 15º, a B, seven 15ºs, and half of the clasp. Sew through the first 15º of the seven, pick up an A, and sew through the 15º, pearl, and 15º in the previous loop **[fig. 5]**. Retrace the thread path, and end the thread (Basics). Repeat with the tail.

Design Option

Use extra beads to make a pair of earrings. For each earring: On 1 yd. (.9 m) of thread, pick up a 15º, a color A 3 mm bicone, a 15º, a 3 mm round pearl, a 15º, an A, a 15º, a color B 3 mm bicone, a 15º, an A, a 15º, a pearl, a 15º, and an A. Sew back through the first 15º to make a loop. Pick up seven 15ºs, and sew back though the 15º your thread exited at the start of this step. Retrace the thread path, and end the thread (Basics). Open a jump ring (Basics), and attach the earring finding to the seed bead loop.

Antique Lace

This technique produces
a lovely, lacy bracelet.

MATERIALS

For a 7-in. (18 cm) bracelet

- 4 mm bicone crystals:
  158 color A
  66 color B
- 5 g 11º seed beads
- Fireline 6 lb. test
- Beading needles, #12

Tip Pick out seed beads
that blend into the colors you
choose for your crystals for a
monochromatic look. You can use
a different color in the center of the
bracelet to make a flower accent.

COLORS

Featured bracelet

4 mm bicone crystals: Jonquil
  Satin, Crystal Champagne
11º seed beads: pale blue-
  lined light topaz luster

Design option

3 mm bicone crystals: Garnet,
  Black Diamond Champagne
3 mm round pearls: dark green
15º seed beads: dark bronze

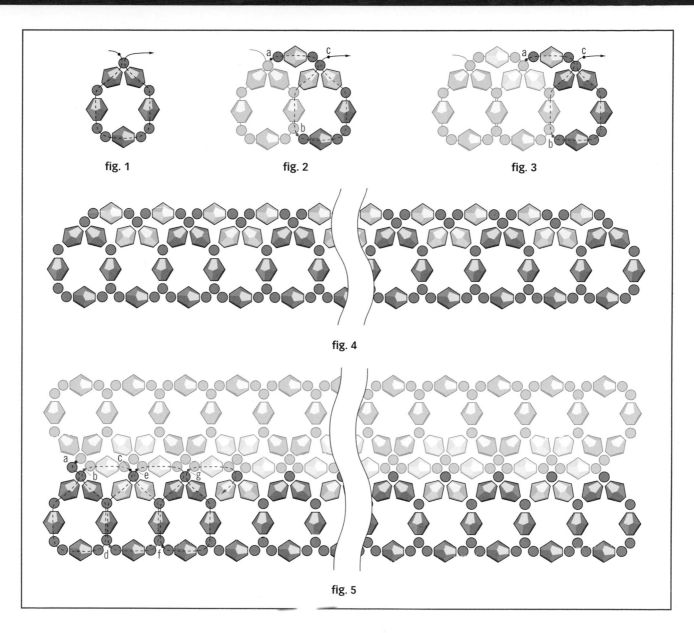

fig. 1

fig. 2

fig. 3

fig. 4

fig. 5

1 On 3 yd. (2.7 m) of Fireline, pick up an 11º, a color A 4 mm bicone crystal, an 11º, an A, two 11ºs, an A, two 11ºs, an A, an 11º, and an A, leaving a 6-in. (15 cm) tail. Sew back through the first 11º strung to form a loop **[fig. 1]**.

2 Pick up an 11º, a color B 4 mm bicone crystal, two 11ºs, and a B. Sew through the side 11º, A, and 11º from the previous step **[fig. 2, a–b]**.

3 Pick up an 11º, an A, two 11ºs, an A, an 11º, and a B. Sew through the 11º above the B from the previous step **[b–c]**.

4 Pick up an 11º, a B, two 11ºs, and an A. Sew through the side 11º, A, and 11º from the previous step **[fig. 3, a–b]**.

5 Pick up an 11º, an A, two 11ºs, an A, an 11º, and an A. Sew through the 11º above the A from the previous step **[b–c]**.

6 Repeat steps 2–5 until you reach your desired length. End on step 5 to preserve the pattern, as shown **[fig. 4]**.

7 Work the second side by repeating steps 1–6, but in step 1, start by picking up two 11ºs. The rest of the step remains the same **[fig. 5, a–b]**. In step 2, sew through the existing 11º, B, and 11º **[b–c]** before picking up an 11º and a B. Then sew through the side 11º, A, and 11º **[c–d]**. Step 3 remains the same **[d–e]**. In step 4, sew through the existing 11º, B, and 11º before picking up an 11º and an A. Then sew through the side 11º, A, and 11º **[e–f]**. Step 5 remains the same **[f–g]**.

8 When you reach the other end, make a loop for the clasp: Pick up an 11º, and sew through the opposite 11º, A, 11º, A, and 11º **[fig. 6, a–b]**. Alternate an 11º and an A six times, and pick up one more 11º. Sew through the end five beads on the opposite side of the bracelet **[b–c]**. Reinforce the loop, and end the thread and tail (Basics).

9 On a new 2-yd. (1.8 m) thread (Basics), pick up an 11º, an A, an 11º, an A, an 11º, and an A. Sew through all six beads again and continue through the first 11º to make a tight ring **[fig. 7]**.

10 Pick up five 11ºs, skip the next crystal, and sew through the next 11º in the ring. Repeat two more times. Sew through the first three 11ºs to step up to the next round **[fig. 8]**. You don't have to reinforce the seed bead round, but you can if you want to make your toggle bar sturdier.

11 Pick up an A, skip five 11ºs, and sew through the next 11º. Repeat two more times **[fig. 9]**. When you complete this round, it will bring the seed bead round close to the crystals. Reinforce this round, and exit an 11º.

12 Repeat steps 10 and 11 until you have eight seed bead rounds and nine crystal rounds.

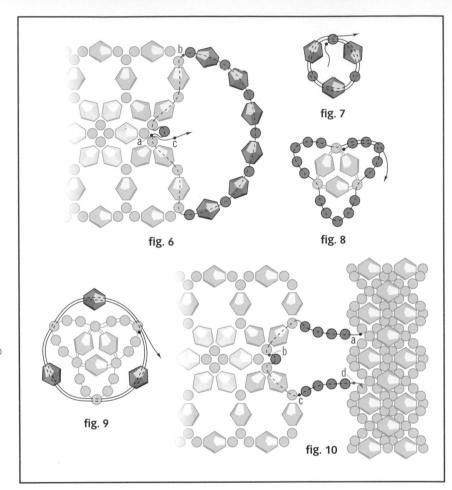

fig. 6

fig. 7

fig. 8

fig. 9

fig. 10

13 Sew to the center rounds on the toggle bar. Pick up four 11ºs, and sew through an 11º, an A, and an 11º on one side of the bracelet **[fig. 10, a–b]**. Pick up an 11º, and sew through the next 11º, A, and 11º **[b–c]**. Pick up four 11ºs, and sew back into the toggle **[c–d]**. Reinforce the connection, and end the thread.

Design Option

For a smaller bracelet, I substituted 3 mm crystals for the 4 mm crystals, and added a Swarovski 3 mm pearl for an accent bead. I used 15º seed beads instead of 11ºs.

Fairy Dust

Glittering snowflakes or something more magical?
Link crystal components into a fabulous bracelet.

MATERIALS

For an 8-in. (20 cm) bracelet

- 64 4 mm bicone crystals, color A
- 28 4 mm bicone crystals, color B
- 168 3 mm bicone crystals
- 2 g 11º cylinder beads
- 10 g 15º seed beads
- Clasp
- 2 jump rings
- Fireline 6 lb. test
- Beading needles, #12
- 2 pairs of pliers

1 On 2 yd. (1.8 m) of Fireline, pick up eight cylinder beads, leaving a 6-in. (15 cm) tail. Sew through the first bead again, forming a ring. Sew through the ring again, skipping every other cylinder, forming a diamond. Exit a corner cylinder **[fig. 1]**.

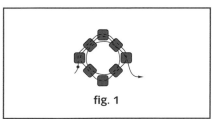

fig. 1

Starlight

Why wait to wish upon the first star you see in the night sky? Create a string of two-sided stars to encircle your wrist.

MATERIALS

For an 8½-in. (21.6 cm) bracelet

- 160 3 mm bicone crystals
- 65 4 mm bicone crystals
- 1 g 15º seed beads
- Clasp
- 2 jump rings
- Fireline 6 lb. test
- Beading needles, #12
- 2 pairs of pliers

1 On 2 yd. (1.8 m) of Fireline, pick up an alternating pattern of three 15ºs and a 4 mm bicone crystal five times, leaving a 12-in. (30 cm) tail. Sew through all the beads again to form a ring, and exit a middle 15º **[fig. 1]**.

2 Pick up five 15ºs, and sew through the next middle 15º in the ring **[fig. 2, a–b]**. Repeat around the ring, and step up through the first three new 15ºs **[b–c]**.

3 Pick up a 3 mm bicone crystal, and sew through the middle 15º in the next set of five 15ºs **[fig. 3, a–b]**. Repeat around **[b–c]**. Reinforce the inner ring of 3 mms and 15ºs, and then sew through the beadwork to exit a middle 15º in the original ring.

4 Repeat steps 2 and 3 on the other side of the ring. Sew through the beadwork to exit an edge 4 mm.

5 Pick up a pattern of three 15ºs and a 4 mm four times, then pick up three 15ºs. Sew through the 4 mm your thread exited at the start of this step. Sew through all the beads again, exiting a middle 15º [**fig. 4**].

6 Repeat steps 2–4 to complete the next star. Sew through the beadwork to exit a 4 mm across from the 4 mm connecting the first two stars. Since the stars have five points, each star will alternate with one 4mm on one edge and two on the other edge [**fig. 5**].

7 Repeat steps 5–6, staggering the stars. Repeat until you complete the desired number of stars (my bracelet has 16), minus the length of the clasp.

8 Exit a middle 15º in the last star. Pick up 11 15ºs, and sew through the middle 15º again. Reinforce the ring, skipping every third bead to make a square-shaped loop [**fig. 6**]. End the thread (Basics). Repeat on the other end with the tail.

9 Open a jump ring (Basics), attach half of the clasp to one of the end loops, and close the ring. Repeat on the other end.

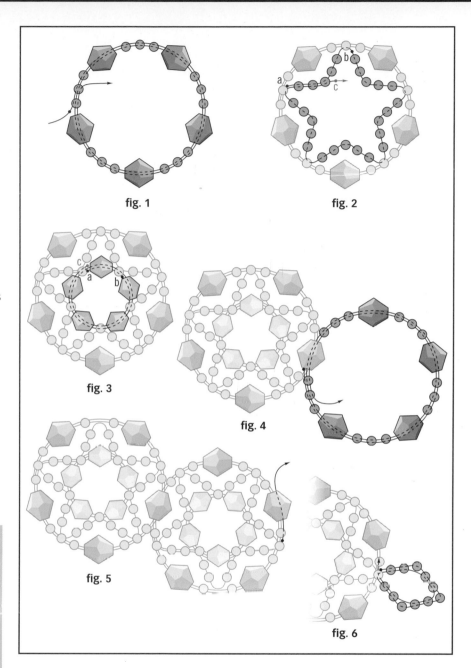

fig. 1

fig. 2

fig. 3

fig. 4

fig. 5

fig. 6

Featured bracelet
4 mm bicone crystals: Erinite AB
3 mm bicone crystals: Pacific Opal
15º seed beads: metallic green iris

Design option
4 mm bicone crystals: Violet
3 mm bicone crystals: Violet Opal
15º seed beads: higher metallic dragonfly

COLORS

Tip Lay out the bracelet often to make sure it's straight as you begin each new component.

Design Option

Add a loop of 15ºs, and you can attach a sparkling star charm to almost anything. Make a pair of stars for a matching set of earrings: Just attach earring findings.

Belle

In this bracelet, loops of flat peyote intertwine with crystal strands. The clasp flows naturally from the loops.

MATERIALS

For a 7½-in. (19.1 cm) bracelet

- 9 5 mm crystal pearls
- 42 4 mm bicone crystals, color A
- 20 4 mm bicone crystals, color B
- 5 g 11º seed beads
- 5 g 11º cylinder beads
- 5 g 15º seed beads
- 80 3 mm bicone crystals
- Crimp bead and crimp cover
- ½ in. (1.3 cm) of small-link chain
- Fireline 6 lb. test
- Flexible beading wire, .014
- Beading needles, #12 or #13
- Crimping pliers
- Wire cutters

1 On 3 yd. (2.7 m) of Fireline, pick up a 5 mm pearl, then pick up an alternating pattern of one 11 cylinder bead and one 15º seed bead until you have 18 cylinders and 17 15ºs. Sew through the 5 mm and the first cylinder again, leaving a 15-in. (38 cm) tail **[fig. 1]**.

2 Work a round of flat, circular peyote (Basics) using cylinders. Step up through the first cylinder added in the new round **[fig. 2]**.

3 Work another round of flat, circular peyote using 11º seed beads. After you complete the round, exit the 5 mm **[fig. 3]**.

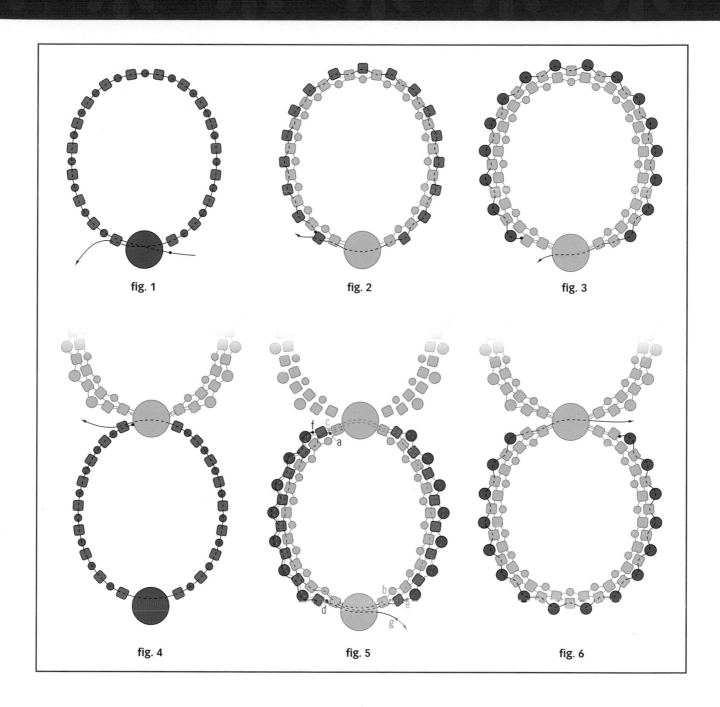

fig. 1

fig. 2

fig. 3

fig. 4

fig. 5

fig. 6

4 Pick up an alternating pattern of a cylinder and a 15º until you have nine cylinders and eight 15ºs. Pick up a 5 mm, then pick up an alternating pattern of a cylinder and a 15º to mirror the first side of the loop. Sew through the 5 mm in the first peyote loop and the first cylinder in the new loop **[fig. 4]**.

5 Work eight stitches in flat, circular peyote using cylinders, then sew through the 5 mm and the next cylinder **[fig. 5, a–b]**. Repeat **[b–c]**. Step up through the first cylinder added in the previous round, and work seven stitches with 11ºs **[c–d]**. Sew through the next cylinder, 5 mm, and two cylinders **[d–e]**, and work seven more stitches with

11ºs **[e–f]**. Sew through the beadwork to exit the bottom 5 mm **[f–g]**.

6 Repeat steps 4 and 5 to make as many peyote loops as needed to reach your desired length, but in the last loop, omit the 5 mm, making it a mirror image of the first loop **[fig. 6]**. End the working thread (Basics).

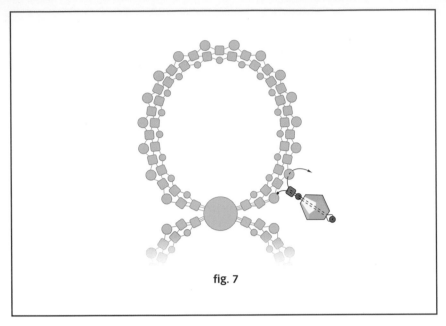

fig. 7

a

b

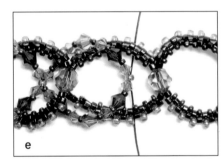

c

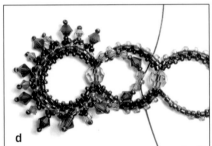

d

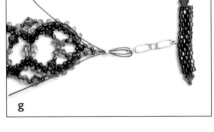

e

f

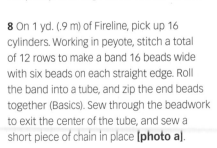

g

7 With the tail, sew through the beadwork to exit the first 11º in the end loop. Pick up a cylinder, a 15º, a 4 mm crystal, and a 15º. Sew back through the 4 mm, the 15º, and the cylinder, and sew through the next 11º in the ring **[fig. 7]**. Repeat around the ring. You can sew an additional row of cylinders along the top of the embellished loop of the clasp loop to strengthen it. End the thread.

8 On 1 yd. (.9 m) of Fireline, pick up 16 cylinders. Working in peyote, stitch a total of 12 rows to make a band 16 beads wide with six beads on each straight edge. Roll the band into a tube, and zip the end beads together (Basics). Sew through the beadwork to exit the center of the tube, and sew a short piece of chain in place **[photo a]**.

9 If desired, add a decorative crystal on each end of the toggle bar **[photo b]**. End the thread.

10 Center a 24-in. (61 cm) length of beading wire in the 5 mm connector bead next to the clasp loop. On each strand, string a 15º, a 3 mm, a 15º, a 3 mm, a 15º, a 3 mm, a 15º, a color A 4 mm, a 15º, and a 3 mm. Bring

the strands over the top of the first loop, and cross the strands through an 11º **[photo c]**. Put both strands through the first loop so the strands are behind the bracelet **[photo d]**.

11 On each strand, pick up a 3 mm, a 15º, an A 4 mm, a 15º, a 3 mm, a 15º, a color D 4 mm, a 15º, a 3 mm, a 15º, an A 4 mm, a 15º, and a 3 mm. Bring the strands over the

Featured bracelet
5 mm round pearls: purple
4 mm bicone crystals: Purple
  Velvet (color A), Indicolite
  AB 2X (color B)
3 mm bicone crystals: Jet Glacier
  Blue 2X
11º seed beads: silver-lined purple
11º cylinder beads: metallic blue iris
15º seed beads: blue iris

Design option
11º seed beads: metallic forest
  green iris
11º hex-cut cylinder beads:
  metallic smoky gold iris
15º seed beads: silver-lined gold
3 mm round pearls: burgundy
3 mm bicone crystals: Khaki
3 mm round crystals: Khaki

Tip Depending on the tension of the peyote rings, you may have to adjust the number of beads you use when crossing the crystal strands through them.

top of the second loop, cross the strands through an 11º, and put the strands through the next loop so the strands are behind the bracelet **[photo e]**.

12 Repeat from step 11 until you reach the last loop. Put the strands behind the bracelet as before, but pick up only a 3 mm, a 15º, an 11º, a 15º, a cylinder, and a 15º. Take each strand through an 11º along the outside of the last loop **[photo f]**. Pick up a 15º, an 11º, and a 15º on each strand. Put both strands through an 11º and a crimp bead, the end link on the chain of the toggle, and back through the crimp bead **[photo g]**. Crimp the crimp bead and trim the tails. Close a crimp cover around the crimp bead.

Design Option

In this green-and-gold variation, I used round 3 mm crystals in a single color instead of bicones. The rounds create a pleasing design with soft lines.

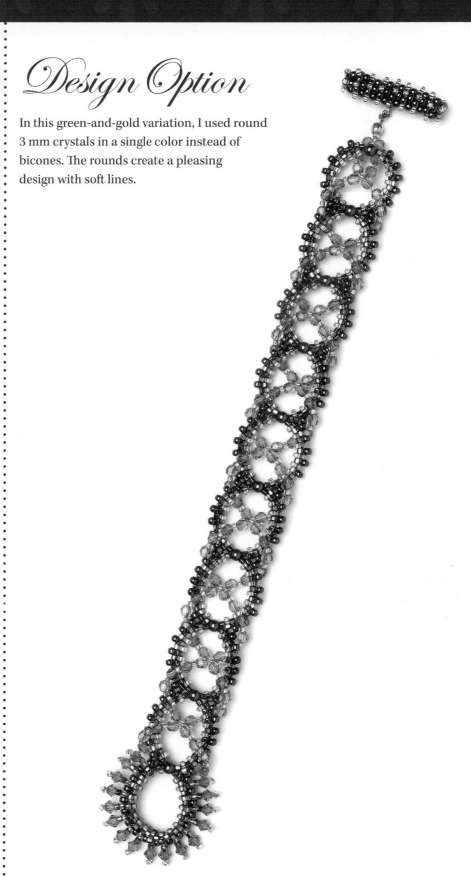

Coquette

Separated by helix crystals, these playful beaded beads link up to form a flirty bracelet.

MATERIALS

For an 8-in. (20 cm) bracelet

- 7–8 8 mm helix crystals
- 14–16 4 mm bicone crystals
- 144–168 3 mm bicone crystals
- 4 g 11º cylinder beads
- 3 g 15º seed beads
- Clasp
- 2 crimp beads
- Fireline 6 lb. test
- Flexible beading wire, .014
- Beading needles, #12
- Crimping pliers
- Wire cutters

1 On 2 yd. (1.8 m) of Fireline, pick up 12 cylinder beads, leaving a 6-in. (15 cm) tail. Sew through the beads again to form a ring, then reinforce, skipping every third cylinder to create four points. Exit a point cylinder **[fig. 1]**.

2 Pick up a 15º, a 3 mm crystal, and a 15º, and sew through the next point cylinder. Repeat three times **[fig. 2]**. Reinforce this round, and exit a point cylinder. This completes the first side.

3 Pick up a cylinder, sew through the cylinder your thread is exiting again, and continue through the new cylinder **[fig. 3]**. This is where the next side will connect.

4 Pick up 11 cylinders and sew through the cylinder the thread is exiting, then reinforce as in step 1 **[fig. 4]**.

5 Add a 15º, a 3 mm, and a 15º between each corner as in step 2, then repeat step 3 **[fig. 5]**.

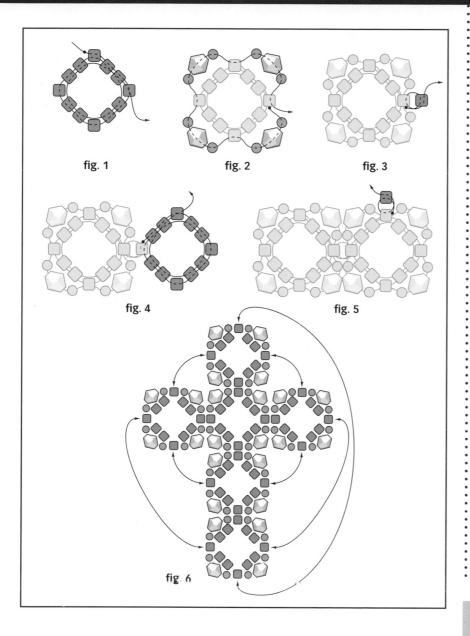

fig. 1

fig. 2

fig. 3

fig. 4

fig. 5

fig. 6

Design Option

Make earrings to match. For each earring, make a beaded bead as in steps 1–6. On a head pin, string a beaded bead, a 15,º a 6 mm, and a 15º. Make a plain or wrapped loop (Basics) above the last 15º strung. Open the loop of an earring finding (Basics), and attach it to the wrapped loop.

6 Repeat steps 4–5 until you have six sides as shown in **fig. 6**. Connect the exposed point cylinders to each other to form the cube. Reinforce as needed to strengthen the cube. End the threads (Basics). Repeat steps 1–6 to make the desired number of crystal cubes (my bracelet has six).

7 Cut 12 in. (30 cm) of beading wire, and string a 4 mm, a 15º, an 8 mm helix crystal, a 15º, a 4 mm, and a crystal cube. If desired, string approximately six cylinders, and slide them inside the cube to cover the wire.

Repeat the pattern until your bracelet is the desired length (you may have to adjust the number of crystals or crystal cubes).

8 On one end of the wire, string a 15º, a crimp bead, and half of the clasp. Go back through the crimp bead, crimp it (Basics), and trim the wire. Repeat at the other end.

Tip Use contrasting colors to make the crystals stand out.

Featured bracelet

8 mm helix crystals: Aquamarine
4 mm bicone crystals: Purple Velvet
3 mm bicone crystals: Light Azore
11º cylinder beads: matte metallic iris
15º seed beads: blue iris

Design option

6 mm bicone crystals: Crystal Silver Shade
3 mm bicone crystals: Olivine
11º cylinder beads: metallic green iris

COLORS

Section Three

GEOMETRIC

Designed to shine in the bright lights of cities big or small,
these projects reveal the edgier side of crystals.

Metropolitan

This bracelet is geared for the newer beader. It's a good example of an easy technique that stitches up into jewelry with a lot of impact.

MATERIALS

For an 8½-in. (21.6 cm) bracelet

- 47 6 mm bicone crystals, color A
- 40 6 mm bicone crystals, color B
- 3 g 11º seed beads
- Two-strand clasp
- Fireline 6–8 lb. test
- Beading needles, #12

Tip Retrace the thread path through the entire band if your tension isn't tight enough.

1 On 3 yd. (2.7 m) of Fireline, pick up a color A 6 mm crystal and an 11º, leaving a 10-in. (25 cm) tail. Sew back through the A. Pick up an 11º and a color B 6 mm crystal four times. Sew back through the first 11º, making a loop of Bs **[fig. 1]**.

2 Pick up an A, an 11º, an A, an 11º, and an A. Sew back through the side 11º in the previous loop **[fig. 2]**.

3 Pick up an A, an 11º, an A, an 11º, and a B. Sew back through the side 11º in the previous loop **[fig. 3]**.

4 Pick up a B, an 11º, a B, an 11º, and a B. Sew back through the side 11º in the previous loop **[fig. 4]**.

5 Pick up an A, an 11º, an A, an 11º, and an A. Sew back through the side 11º in the previous loop **[fig. 5]**.

6 Pick up an A, an 11º, an A, an 11º, and a B. Sew back through the side 11º in the previous loop **[fig. 6]**.

fig. 1   **fig. 2**   **fig. 3**   **fig. 4**

fig. 5   **fig. 6**

fig. 7   **flg. 8**

7 Pick up a B, an 11º, a B, an 11º, and a B. Sew back through the side 11º in the previous loop **[fig. 7]**.

8 Repeat steps 2–7 until you have 10 color B units.

9 To complete the band, pick up an A and a 15º, and sew back through the A **[fig. 8, a–b]**.

10 Sew back through the previous 15º, and pick up three 15ºs and one loop of the clasp **[b–c]**. Sew back through the four 15ºs, and continue through the next B and 15º **[c–d]**. Pick up one 15º and the other clasp loop, and sew back through the two 15ºs and the next B **[d–e]**. Retrace the thread path to reinforce the connection, and end the thread (Basics)

11 With the tail, work as in step 10 to connect the other clasp half at the other end.

Design Option

This bracelet looks adorable in a smaller size. Try substituting 3 or 4 mm crystals for the 6 mms and pearls for the color B crystals.

Cubist

Create crystal quatrefoils with right-angle weave, and capture every other one in a bugle-bead frame to make this bracelet.

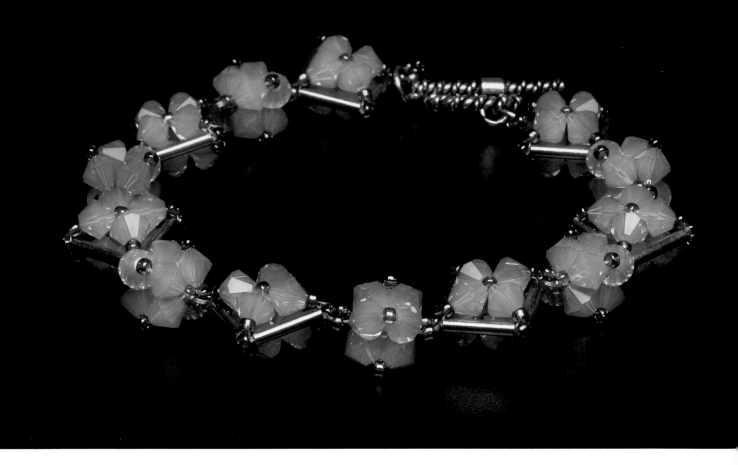

MATERIALS

For an 8½-in. (21.6 cm) bracelet

- 28 12 mm bugle beads
- 76 5 mm bicone crystals
- 4 g 11º seed beads
- Clasp
- 2 4 mm jump rings
- Fireline 6 lb. test
- Beading needles, #12 or 13
- 2 pairs of pliers

1 On 2 yd. (1.8 m) of Fireline, pick up a repeating pattern of an 11º seed bead and a 12 mm bugle bead four times, leaving a 6-in. (15 cm) tail. Sew through all the beads again to form a ring, and exit the first 11º **[fig. 1]**.

2 Pick up an 11º, a 5 mm bicone crystal, an 11º, a 5 mm, and an 11º. Sew through the next 11º in the ring, and back through the last 11º, 5 mm, and 11º **[fig. 2]**.

3 Pick up a 5 mm and an 11º, and sew through the opposite 11º in the ring. Sew back through the last 11º, 5 mm, and 11º. Repeat, sewing through the remaining 11º

in the ring **[fig. 3]**. Sew through the beadwork to exit an edge 11º in the bugle ring.

4 Pick up three 11ºs, and sew back through the 11º your thread exited at the start of this step. Retrace the thread path, and exit the opposite 11º **[fig. 4]**.

5 Pick up a repeating pattern of a 5 mm and an 11º three times, and pick up a 5 mm. Sew through the 11º your thread exited at the start of this step, retrace the thread path, and exit the opposite 11º **[fig. 5]**.

6 Add a second layer of crystals to the previous step by picking up a 5 mm, an

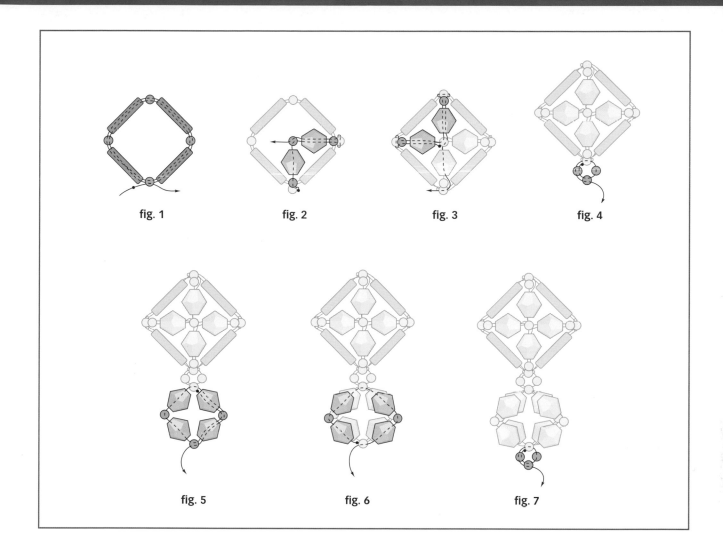

fig. 1 fig. 2 fig. 3 fig. 4

fig. 5 fig. 6 fig. 7

11º, and a 5 mm. Sew through the opposite 11º from the previous step. Repeat **[fig. 6]**. Retrace the thread path, and exit the end 11º.

7 Pick up three 11ºs, and sew through the 11º your thread exited at the start of this step. Retrace the thread path, and exit the opposite 11º **[fig. 7]**.

Tip Discard any sharp or uneven bugle beads. Before you make each bugle component, choose four bugles and place them next to each other to ensure the component will be even.

Featured bracelet
12 mm bugle beads:
  nickel plated
5 mm bicone crystals:
  Pacific Opal
11º seed beads: gold luster
  blue/green

Design option
15 mm bugle beads: teal AB
6 mm bicone crystals: Light Azore
11º seed beads: lined rainbow AB

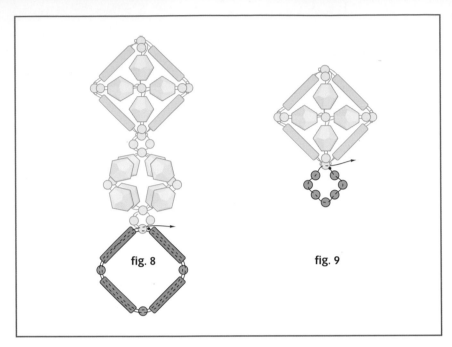

fig. 8

fig. 9

8 Pick up a bugle and an 11º three times, then pick up a bugle. Sew through the 11º your thread exited at the start of this step. Retrace the thread path **[fig. 8]**.

9 Repeat steps 2–8 until you have seven bugle units.

10 Exiting the end 11º, pick up seven 11ºs, and sew through the end 11º again **[fig. 9]**. Retrace the thread path, and end the thread (Basics). Repeat on the other end.

11 Open a jump ring (Basics), attach half a clasp to an end loop, and close the jump ring. Repeat on the other end.

Design Option

Use smaller or larger bugles with larger or smaller crystals for different sized units. This pendant uses 12 mm bugles with 6 mm crystals.

Want to use pearls? Omit the second layer of the beaded bead unit (step 6).

XOXO

Nestle crystals between rows of netted bugle beads for a bangle that is stackable, sparkling fun.

MATERIALS

For a 7¾-in. (19.7 cm) bangle

- 70 4 mm bicone crystals
- 35 4 mm round crystals
- 35 3 mm pearls
- 10 g 3 mm bugle beads
- 5 g 11º seed beads
- 5 g 15º seed beads
- Fireline 6 or 8 lb. test
- Beading needles, #12 or #13

COLORS

Featured bangle

4 mm round crystals: Tanzanite
3 mm pearls: dark purple
3 mm bugle beads: blue iris
11º seed beads: blue iris
15º seed beads: lined purple

Design option—bangle

4 mm pearls: light gray
3 mm pearls: light gray
3 mm bugle beads: matte silver
11º and 15º seed beads: silver

Design option—pendant

6 mm bicone crystals:
   Crystal Starlight
3 mm bugle beads: matte
   metallic silver
3 mm pearls: gray

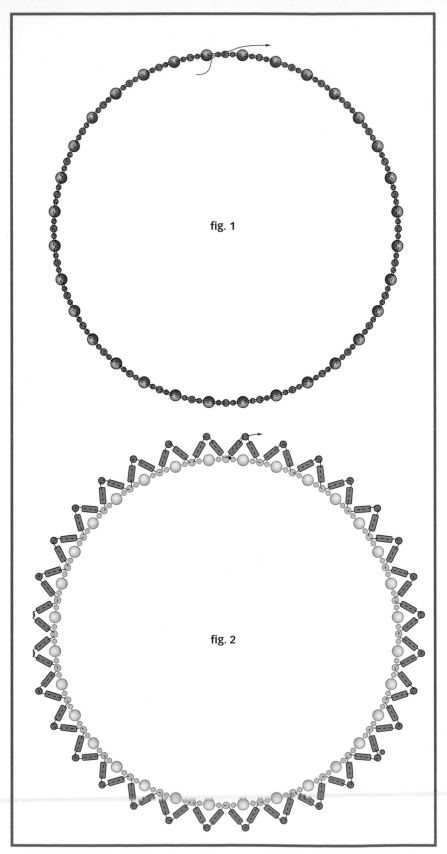

fig. 1

fig. 2

1 String a stop bead (Basics) to the middle of 4 yd. (3.6 m) of Fireline. On one end, pick up a repeating pattern of a 15º seed bead, an 11º seed bead, a 15º, and a 3 mm pearl until you have enough beads to fit around the largest part of your hand. Sew through all the beads again to form a ring, exiting the first 11º **[fig. 1]**.

2 Pick up a 3 mm bugle, an 11º, and a bugle, and sew through the next 11º in the ring. Repeat around the ring and exit an 11º in the new round **[fig. 2]**. Remove the stop bead, thread a needle on the tail, and repeat for a second round of netting off the ring.

3 Pick up a 15º, a 4 mm bicone crystal, and a 15º. Sew through the next 11º on the same side. Repeat to add a 15º, 4 mm, and a 15º between each netting stitch **[fig. 3]**. Use the other tail to repeat on the other side.

4 Exiting an 11º between 4 mms, pick up a bugle, an 11º, and a bugle. Sew through the next 11º on the same side **[fig. 4, a–b]**. Repeat to add a second netted round on one side.

5 Using the other tail, exit an 11º between 4 mms on the other side. Pick up a bugle, and sew through the corresponding 11º on the first side **[c–d]**. Pick up another bugle, and sew through the next11º on the second side **[d–e]**. Complete the round.

6 Exiting an 11º in the outer center ring, pick up a 15º, a 4 mm round, and a 15º. Sew through the next center round 11º **[fig. 5]**. Complete the round.

7 Retrace the thread path, and end the threads (Basics).

Tip If you have trouble keeping the bugles in a diamond shape, sew through the bugle round again, skipping the 11ºs.

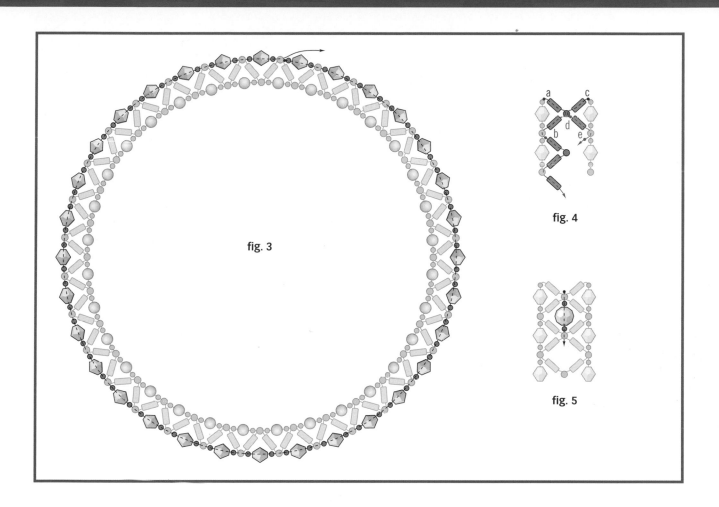

fig. 3

fig. 4

fig. 5

Design Options

After you stitch up the crystal version, try a bangle that uses crystal pearls along the inner and outer ring. Another option using 3 mm pearls is this pendant; stitch it in the same manner as the bangle, but with these changes:

1 For the inner ring, pick up a pattern of a 15º, an 11º, a 15º, and a 3 mm pearl eight times.

2 Work a bugle round as in step 2 of the bangle.

3 Work a crystal round with a 15º, a 6 mm, and a 15º.

4 Work a bugle round.

5 Work steps 2 and 3 on the other side of the pendant.

6 Work a bugle round as in step 5 of the bangle.

7 Work the outer 6 mm round.

8 To make a hanging loop, pick up a 15º, a bugle, a 15º, and an 11º three times, then pick up a 15º, a bugle, and a 15º. Make a loop, and end the threads.

Sputnik

Intersperse these spunky beaded beads with crystal rondelles for a bracelet with big impact.

MATERIALS

For each beaded bead

- 12 4 mm round crystals
- 8 4 mm bicone crystals
- 4 3 mm bicone crystals
- 1 g 15º seed beads
- Fireline 6 lb. test
- Beading needles, #12 or 13

For an 8¼-in. (21 cm) bracelet

- 7 beaded beads: 4 using color A 4 mm rounds and color C 3 mm bicones, and 3 using color B rounds and color D 3 mm bicones

- 8 8 mm crystal rondelles
- 8 4 mm rounds
- 6 4 mm bicones
- 16 3 mm bicones
- 1 g 15º seed beads
- Toggle clasp
- 2 crimp beads
- 2 crimp covers (optional)
- Flexible beading wire, .014
- Crimping pliers
- Wire cutters

Tip You can make fewer beaded beads and string more accent beads between each beaded bead.

1 On 2 yd. (1.8 m) of Fireline, pick up four 4 mm round crystals, leaving a 6-in. (15 cm) tail. Sew through the first three crystals again to form a tight ring **[fig. 1]**.

2 Pick up three 4 mm round crystals, and sew through the 4 mm your thread is exiting from the last step. Sew through the next two new 4 mm round crystals **[fig. 2]**.

3 Repeat step 2 **[fig. 3]**.

4 Pick up a 4 mm round crystal, and sew through the opposite end 4 mm. Pick up another 4 mm, and sew through the crystal your thread exited in step 3 **[fig. 4]**.

5 Pick up a 15º, a 3 mm bicone crystal, and a 15º. Sew through the opposite 4 mm round

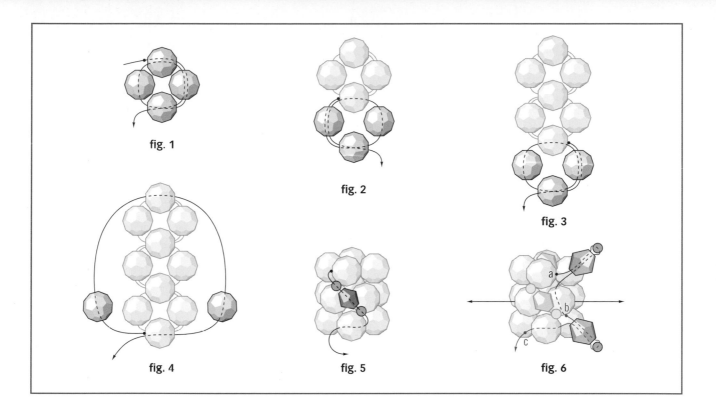

fig. 1

fig. 2

fig. 3

fig. 4

fig. 5

fig. 6

crystal, going in the same direction. The 3 mm will lie diagonally across one of the cubes' sides **[fig. 5]**. Repeat three times, leaving a hole in the center of the beaded bead.

6 Add spikes to each corner of the beaded bead: Pick up a 4 mm bicone and a 15º. Skip the 15º, and sew back through the 4 mm bicone. Sew through the next 4 mm round, exiting the next corner **[fig. 6, a–b]**. Repeat **[b–c]** around the beaded bead, adding a spike at all eight corners. After all of the spikes are added, retrace the thread path, making a firm beaded bead. End the threads (Basics).

7 Repeat steps 1–6 to make a total of seven beaded beads.

8 To make a bracelet, string a pattern of a 3 mm bicone, an 8 mm rondelle, a 3 mm, a 4 mm round, a beaded bead, a 4 mm round, a 3 mm, an 8 mm, a 3 mm, a 4 mm bicone,

a beaded bead, and a 4 mm bicone. Repeat the pattern until you've strung all seven beaded beads and eight 8 mm rondelles. End with a 3 mm bicone.

9 on one end, string a crimp bead and one half of the clasp. Go back through the crimp bead, crimp it (Basics), and trim the wire. Repeat on the other end. If desired, close a crimp cover around each crimp bead.

Featured bracelet
8 mm crystal rondelles: Light Colorado Topaz
4 mm round crystals: Crystal Dorado (color A), Crystal Golden Shadow (color B)
4 mm bicone crystals: Olivine Vitrail
3 mm bicone crystals: Khaki (color C), Crystal Dorado 2X (color D)
15º seed beads: gold-lined rainbow black diamond

COLORS

Design Option

For earrings, make a beaded bead as in steps 1–6. On a headpin, string a 15º, a 3 mm bicone, a beaded bead, a 3 mm, and a 15º, and make a wrapped loop (Basics). Open the loop on an earring finding and attach it to the wrapped loop. Repeat to make a second earring.

Bright Lights

Stained glass windows inspired this beaded bead. Because the underside is flat, it rests comfortably on the wrist.

MATERIALS

For a 7¾-in. (19.7 cm) bracelet

- 86 4 mm bicone crystals
- 54 3 mm bicone crystals
- 2 g 11º seed beads
- 3 g 15º seed beads
- Clasp
- 2 4 mm jump rings
- Fireline 4 or 6 lb. test
- Beading needles, #12 or #13
- 2 pairs of pliers

Featured bracelet and design option

3 and 4 mm bicones: Garnet Satin

11º and 15º seed beads: nickel plated

COLORS

Tip For a lively bracelet, make each component in a different color.

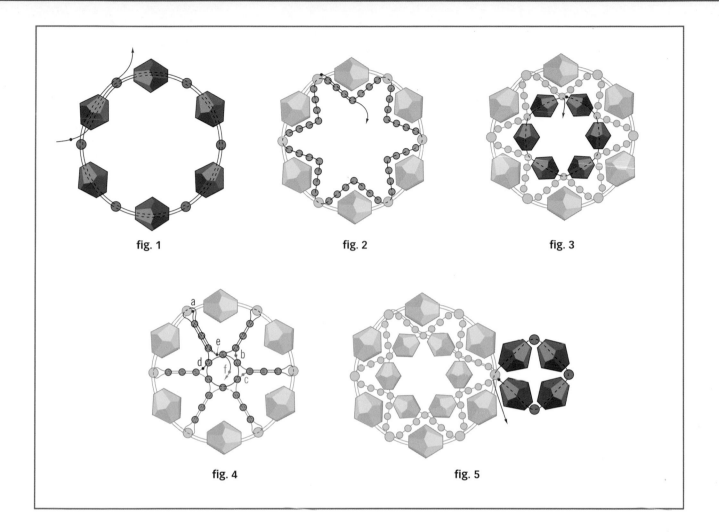

fig. 1

fig. 2

fig. 3

fig. 4

fig. 5

1 On a comfortable length of Fireline, pick up a pattern of a 4 mm bicone crystal and a 11º seed bead six times, leaving a 6-in. (15 cm) tail. Sew through all the beads again to form a ring, and exit the first 11º **[fig. 1]**.

2 Pick up seven 15ºs, and sew through the next 11º in the ring. Repeat to complete the round, and step up through the first four 15ºs in the first stitch **[fig. 2]**.

3 Pick up a 3 mm bicone crystal, skip three 15ºs, an 11º, and three 15ºs, and sew through the next 15º. Repeat to complete the round, and exit a 15º **[fig. 3]**.

4 Sew through the beadwork to exit an 11º in the outer ring. Pick up seven 15ºs, and sew through the next 11º in the ring and back through the last three 15ºs **[fig. 4, a–b]**.

5 Pick up four 15ºs, sew through the next 11º in the ring, and sew back through the last three 15ºs **[b–c]**. Repeat three times **[c–d]**. Pick up a 15º, sew through the first three 15ºs picked up in step 4, the 11º in the ring, and back through the three 15ºs **[d–e]**.

6 Sew through the six 15ºs in the center **[e–f]**.

7 Sew through the beadwork, and exit an 11º in the outer ring. Pick up a repeating pattern of a 4 mm and an 11º three times, then pick up a 4 mm. Sew through the 11º your thread exited at the beginning of this step **[fig. 5]**. Retrace the thread path several times, and exit the 11º opposite the 11º your thread exited at the beginning of this step.

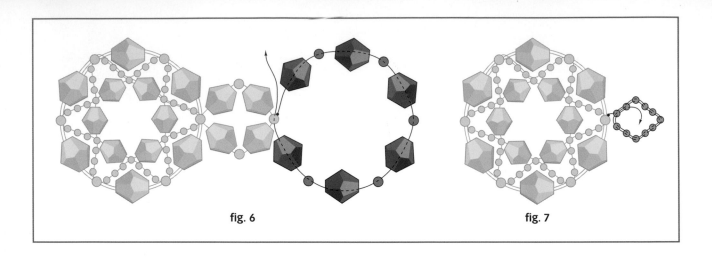

fig. 6   fig. 7

8 Pick up a pattern of a 4 mm bicone and an 11º five times, and then pick up a 4 mm bicone. Sew through the 11º your thread exited at the start of this step **[fig. 6]**.

9 Repeat steps 2–8 until you have nine star-shaped units.

10 Sew though the beadwork to exit the end 11º. Pick up 11 15ºs to make a loop at one end of the bracelet **[fig. 7]**. Retrace the thread path, and end the thread (Basics). Repeat on the other end.

11 Open a 4 mm jump ring (Basics), and attach half a clasp to an end loop. Repeat on the other end.

DesignOption

Make a single beaded component into a sweet ring.

1 Work steps 1–6 to make the ring top.

2 Exit an 11º in the outer ring of beads. Pick up a 15,º two 11ºs, and a 15º, and sew through the edge 11º again. Sew through the first new 15º and two 11ºs.

3 Pick up a 15º, two 11ºs, and a 15º, and sew through the two 11ºs added in the previous step and the first new 15º and two 11ºs. Repeat until the band is long enough to fit around your finger.

4 Pick up a 15º, and sew through the opposite 11º in the outer round of the ring top.

5 Pick up a 15º, and sew through the next side 15º in the band. Repeat until you reach the other end, sew through the beadwork to reach the other side of the band, and add 15ºs on this edge. End the threads (Basics).

Cages

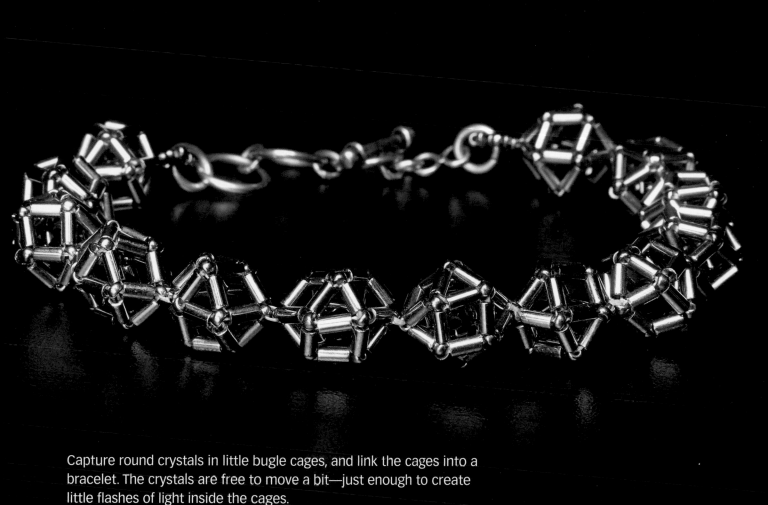

Capture round crystals in little bugle cages, and link the cages into a bracelet. The crystals are free to move a bit—just enough to create little flashes of light inside the cages.

MATERIALS

For a 7¼-in. (18.4 cm) bracelet

- 17 4 mm round crystals
- 10 g 3 mm bugles
- 3 g 15º seed beads
- Clasp
- Fireline 6 lb. test
- Beading needles, #12

1 On 2 yd. (1.8 m) of Fireline, pick up a pattern of a 15º and a bugle four times, leaving a 6-in. (15 cm) tail. Sew through the first 15º again, then sew through the ring a second time, skipping the 15ºs, so the ring forms a square. Exit a 15º **[fig. 1]**.

2 Pick up a bugle, a 15º, a bugle, a 15º, a bugle, a 15º, and a bugle. Sew through the 15º your thread exited at the start of this last step, then sew through the ring again, skipping the 15ºs to form a square. Exit the 15º opposite the point where the first two squares join **[fig. 2]**.

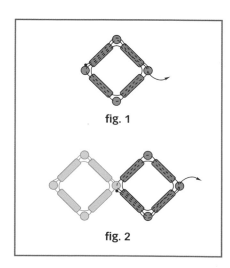

fig. 1

fig. 2

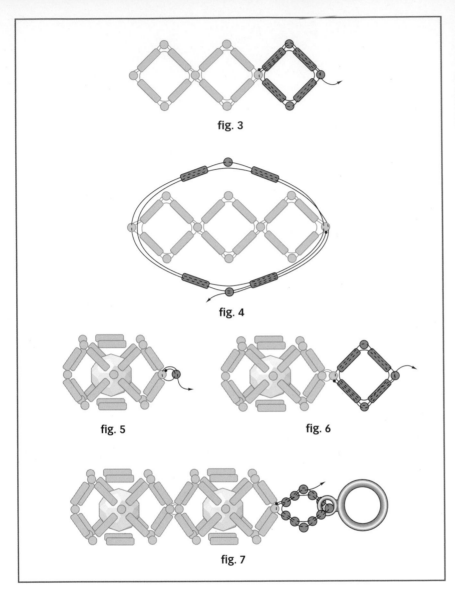

fig. 3

fig. 4

fig. 5

fig. 6

fig. 7

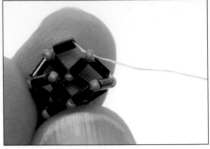

8 Work the next cage off the first: Pick up a bugle, a 15º, a bugle, a 15º, a bugle, a 15º, and a bugle. Sew through the 15º added in the previous step, then sew through the ring again, skipping the 15ºs to form a square. Exit the 15º opposite the joining 15º **[fig. 6]**.

9 Work as in step 8 for two more stitches, then connect the strip into a ring as in step 4. Complete the beaded bead as in steps 5–6.

10 Repeat steps 7–9 until you have the desired number of bugle bead cages (my bracelet has 13).

11 Exiting an end 15º, pick up 11 15ºs and half of the clasp. Sew through the 15º your thread exited at the beginning of this step. Retrace the ring, skipping every third 15º, to mimic the square shape as before **[fig. 7]**. End the tail (Basics). Repeat on the other end with the other half of the clasp.

3 Repeat step 2 **[fig. 3]**.

4 Join the first and last stitch by picking up a bugle, a 15º, and a bugle. Sew through the end 15º in the first stitch. Pick up a bugle, a 15º, and a bugle, and sew through the 15º your thread exited at the start of this step. Sew through the ring a second time, skipping the 15ºs to form a square **[fig. 4]**.

5 The ring of bugle stitches has four 15ºs open on each edge of the band. Exit a 15º on one open edge, pick up a bugle, and sew through the next 15º on the same

end. Repeat three more times, then sew through all the beads again to form a square **[photo]**.

6 Repeat on the other end, but before you reinforce the ring to make a square, push a 4 mm round bead or crystal into the center of the bugle cage. Reinforce the ring to form a square, and exit a 15º.

7 Pick up a 15º, and sew through the 15º in the previous cage and the new 15º **[fig. 5]**.

Featured bracelet
4 mm round crystals: Crystal Vitrail
3 mm bugles: matte silver
15º seed beads: nickel

Design option—teal bracelet
8 mm pearls: Tahitian
4 mm round crystals: Indian Sapphire
3 mm bugles: matte teal iris
15º seed beads: matte teal iris

Design option—bronze bracelet
8 mm round crystal: Khaki
6 mm crystal rondelle: Light Colorado Topaz
4 mm bugles: red copper matte metallic iris
11º seed beads: olive matte metallic

Design option—earrings
3 mm bugles: blue iris
6 mm glass beads: purple
4 mm round crystals: Amethyst
11º seed beads: transparent blue luster

Tip If your tension is loose, a 6 mm round bead inside the bugle cage may be a better fit than a 4 mm bead.

Design Options

Instead of connecting all beaded cages together, alternate pearls or crystals with the cages.

To include beads between the cages, stitch up a handful of cages. Exit any 15º in a cage, pick up a bead (or a group of beads), and sew through a 15º in the next cage. Retrace the thread path a couple of times, and end the thread (Basics). Repeat to connect additional cages.

To make coordinating earrings, make a bugle cage as in steps 1–6, then complete as follows:

1 On the tail, pick up an 11º, a 6 mm, an 11º, a 4 mm, an 11º, and a soldered ring. Skip the ring, and sew back through the rest of the beads picked up in this step. End the thread.

2 Attach an earring finding to the soldered ring, and make a second earring to match.

ORGANIC

These designs were inspired by nature's patterns, forms, and always-harmonious color palette.

Clusters

You'll develop the design of this necklace very organically. Make individual clusters in shapes and size you like, then link them so they lie nicely around the neck.

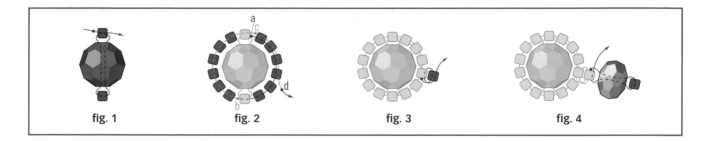

fig. 1   fig. 2   fig. 3   fig. 4

1 On 1 yd. (.9 m) of Fireline, pick up a cylinder, a crystal, and a cylinder, leaving a 6-in. (15 cm) tail. Sew back through the crystal and the cylinder on the opposite end. Your working thread and tail will be exiting opposite sides of the first cylinder **[fig. 1]**.

2 Pick up enough cylinders to sit snugly next to one side of the crystal. Sew though the cylinder at the opposite end of the crystal **[fig. 2, a–b]**.

3 Pick up the same number of cylinders as in step 2, and sew through the cylinder at the opposite end of the crystal **[b–c]**. Sew through the next few cylinders **[c–d]** to offset the position of the next crystal.

4 Pick up a cylinder, and sew through the cylinder your thread exited in step 3 and the new cylinder, so the two cylinders sit tightly next to each other **[fig. 3]**.

5 Pick up a new size and shape of crystal and a cylinder. Sew back through the new crystal and the cylinder your thread exited in step 4 **[fig. 4]**.

MATERIALS

For a 15-in. (38 cm) necklace

- 25–36 4–10 mm crystals, gems, and pearls in assorted colors and a variety of round, oval, and teardrop shapes
- 5–7 g 11º cylinder beads, Charlottes, or three-cuts
- Toggle clasp
- Fireline 6 lb. test
- Beading needles, #12

Tip If you have a hard time keeping the seed-bead rings tight around the crystals, sew through the ring a second time.

COLORS

Featured necklace
6 mm round crystals: Green Iris
6 mm round crystal: Amethyst
6 mm rondelle crystals: Erinite
6 mm cube crystals: Erinite
4 mm round crystals: Amethyst and Erinite
4 mm assorted round glass beads: greens and purples
11º seed beads: matte green iris AB

Bracelet
8 mm faceted pearls: light gray
8 mm round crystals: Light Vitral
6 mm round crystals: Montana, Violet, and Tanzanite
4 mm round crystals: Indian Sapphire, Crystal Ice, and Tanzanite AB
4 mm pearls: light gray
11º seed beads: shimmering capri color-lined midnight blue

5 Use the working thread to add a round of 15ºs to snug the beadwork next to the large bead. Use the tail to work a round of 15ºs on the other side of the base round **[fig. 4]**.

6 Exit a cylinder in the first round. Pick up a cylinder, and sew through the cylinder your thread is exiting. Retrace the thread path, and exit the new cylinder **[fig. 5]**.

7 Pick up a different size or shape crystal and a cylinder. Sew back through the crystal and the cylinder added in the previous step **[fig. 6]**. Repeat steps 2–5 at least seven times, adding a new shape, color, or size of crystal each time. (If you're using 4 or 5 mm beads, a base round of 15ºs or cylinders may be enough to hold the bead.) End the working thread (Basics).

8 Using the tail, sew through the beadwork and exit where you would like to attach the hanging loop. Make a loop of cylinders long enough to accommodate a jump ring. Work a few rounds of peyote stitch (Basics) if desired to strengthen the loop. End the tail **[photo]**.

9 Open a jump ring (Basics), and attach the hanging loop. Close the jump ring. Hang your pendant from a chain or cord.

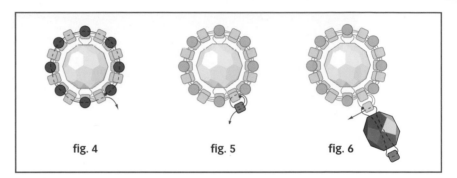

fig. 4   fig. 5   fig. 6

Tip Before you begin to stitch, lay out the assorted crystals on your work surface to determine the general shape of the pendant.

COLORS

Featured pendant
8 mm round crystals: Montana, Tanzanite, and Purple Velvet
8 mm cube crystal: Tanzanite
6 mm bicone crystal: Indian Sapphire
6 mm rondelle crystal: Montana
4 mm round crystals: Montana AB
11º cylinder beads: metallic blue iris
15º seed beads: gray AB

Design option
11º seed beads: nickel plated
8 mm round crystal: Jet
4 mm pearls: light gray

Design Option

Stitch a coordinating Droplets ring:

1 Work steps 1–5 to surround a 6 or 8 mm bead with five rounds of peyote stitch (Basics).

2 Exit a 15º in the center round of peyote. Pick up a 3 mm round pearl, enough 15ºs to surround your finger, and a 3 mm pearl. Sew through a 15º in the center round opposite the 15º your thread is exiting **[photo a]**.

3 Sew back through the pearl, pick up the same number of 15ºs as in step 2, and sew through the opposite 3 mm pearl **[photo b]**.

4 Retrace the thread path to secure the ring bands, and end the thread.

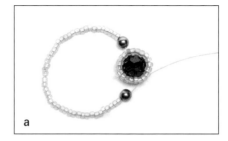

a

b

Aurora

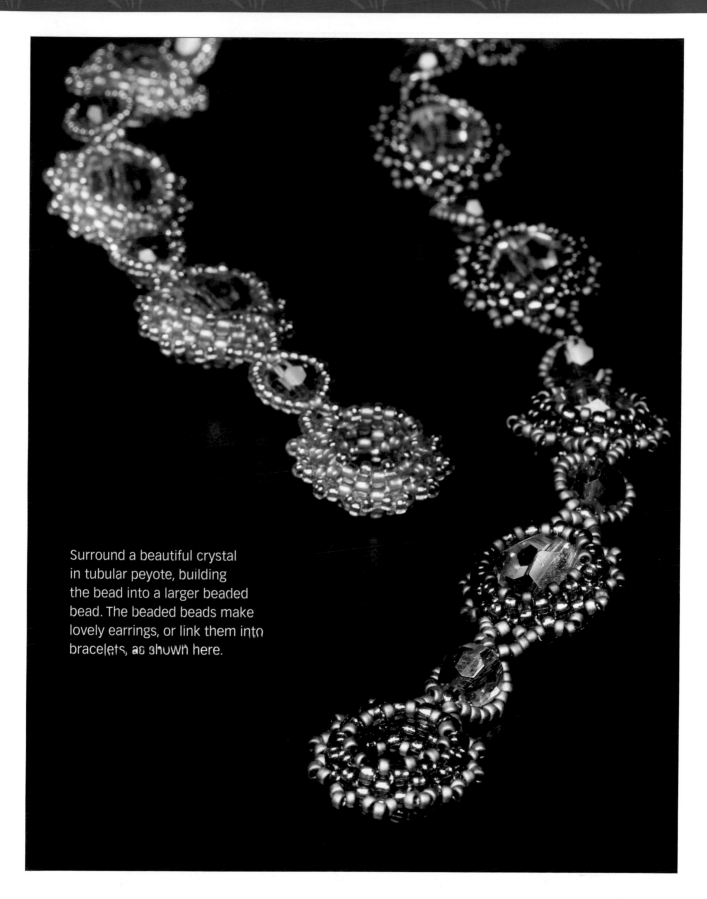

Surround a beautiful crystal in tubular peyote, building the bead into a larger beaded bead. The beaded beads make lovely earrings, or link them into bracelets, as shown here.

Tide Pool

The subtle interplay of water and light inspired this bracelet and its monochromatic color palette. Bicone crystals interlock easily into rings, and the crystal rings are linked by tiny seed-bead rings.

MATERIALS

For an 8-in. (20 cm) bracelet

- 62 4 mm crystals (color A)
- 62 4 mm crystals (color B)
- 5 g 11º seed beads
- 5 g 15º seed beads
- Clasp (toggle bar and four links of large-link chain)
- 2 jump rings
- Fireline 6 lb. test
- Beading needles, #12 or #13
- 2 pairs of pliers

Featured bracelet

4 mm bicone crystals: Jet AB 2X (color A) and Chrysolite (color B)
11º seed beads: lined rainbow AB

Design option

3 mm bicone crystals: Garnet Satin
15º seed beads: nickel plated

COLORS

1 On 2 yd. (1.8 m) of Fireline, pick up a pattern of an 11º and a color A 4 mm six times, leaving a 6-in. (15 cm) tail. Sew through all the beads again to form a tight ring, and exit a 11º **[fig. 1]**.

2 Pick up two 15ºs, an 11º, and two 15ºs, and sew through the next 11º in the ring. Repeat five times, and step up through the first two 15ºs and 11º in the first stitch **[fig. 2]**.

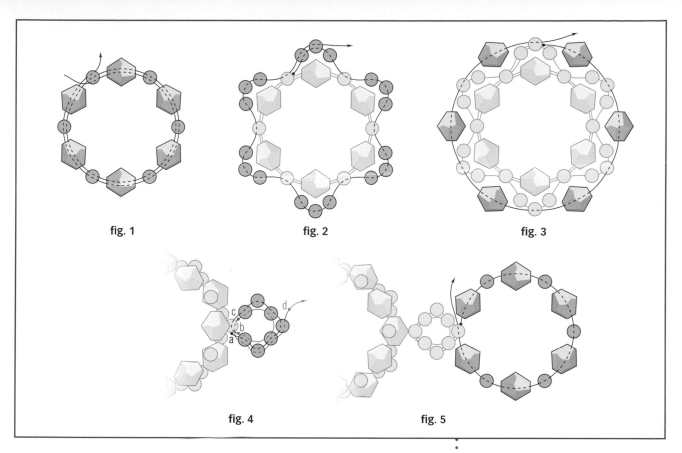

fig. 1   fig. 2   fig. 3

fig. 4   fig. 5

3 Pick up a color B 4 mm, skip five beads in the previous ring, and sew through the next 11º. Repeat five times **[fig. 3]**, pulling tight as you stitch. Reinforce the ring with a second pass of thread.

4 Exit an 11º opposite the tail, positioned between two crystals in the first ring of crystals. Pick up seven 11ºs, and sew through the 11º your thread exited in the ring **[fig. 4, a–b]**. Reinforce the 11ºs, skipping every other 11º in the ring to pull the beads into a square **[b–c]**. You may have to poke the beads on the corners with your needle to get them stick out. Sew through the ring to exit the 15º opposite the previous crystal ring **[c–d]**.

5 Pick up a color A 4 mm and a 15º seven times, and then pick up an A 4 mm. Sew through the 11º your thread exited at the start of this step, and reinforce the ring as in step 1 **[fig. 5]**.

6 Repeat steps 2–5 until you reach the desired finished length, minus the length of the clasp.

7 Pick up seven 11ºs, and sew through the 11º your thread exited at the start of this step. Sew through the beads just picked up, and end the thread (Basics). Repeat on the other end using the tail.

8 Open a jump ring (Basics), and attach the toggle bar to one end. On the other end, open a jump ring and attach the chain link extender.

Design Option

This petite version of the bracelet is made in the same way, substituting 15ºs for 11ºs and 3 mm crystals for 4 mms.

Featherweight

This fluid herringbone necklace drapes beautifully, and the spaces in the base simply beg to be embellished with hundreds of sparkling round and bicone crystals. The pretty shell flower is functional as a closure and also makes a beautiful focal point.

MATERIALS

For an 18-in. (46 cm) necklace

- 180–220 3 mm bicone crystals
- 90–100 2 mm round crystals
- 10 mm flat flower bead
- 10 g 10º cylinder beads
- 5 g 15º seed beads
- Fireline 4 or 6 lb. test
- Beading needles, #12

1 On 2 yd. (1.8 m) of Fireline, pick up two 10º cylinder beads. Leaving a 12-in. (30 cm) tail, sew through both beads again to reinforce the stitch, exiting the first bead **[fig. 1]**.

2 Pick up two 10ºs, and sew down through the second bead in the previous row. Pick up two 15º seed beads, and sew back up through the second 10º picked up in the new row **[fig. 2]**.

3 Working in flat herringbone stitch, repeat step 2 **[fig. 3]** until your band is the desired length. Keep in mind that if your tension isn't

tight enough, your band may shrink as you add the top embellishment row.

4 To add branched fringe, pick up about 38 15ºs, a 3 mm bicone crystal, and three 15ºs. Sew back through the 3 mm and the next six 15ºs **[fig. 4, a–b]**. Pick up five 15ºs, a 3 mm, and three 15ºs, and sew back through the 3 mm, five 15ºs, and the next few 15ºs in the stem **[b–c]**. Repeat several times until you have added fringe all along the stem, varying the length of the branches as desired **[c–d]**. Sew back into the end cylinder, and back through the adjacent cylinder **[d–e]**.

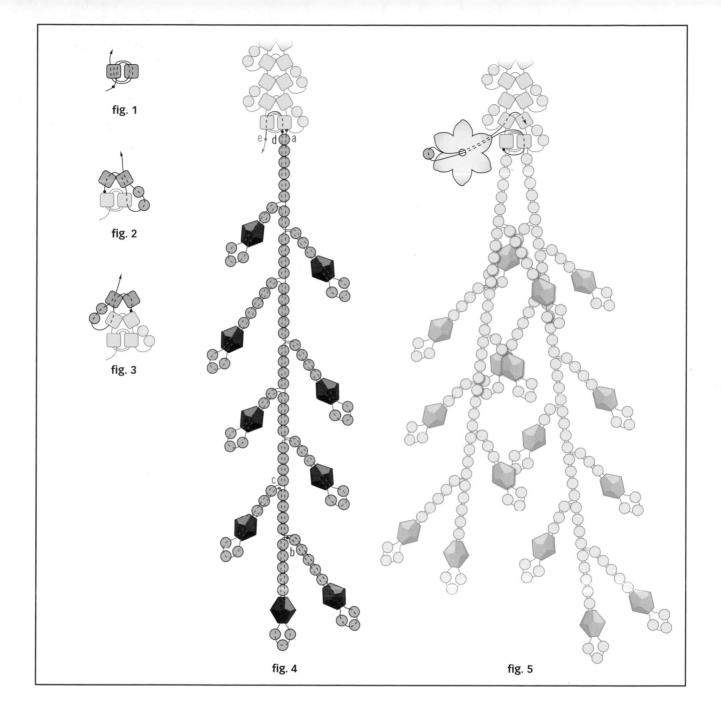

fig. 1

fig. 2

fig. 3

fig. 4

fig. 5

5 Repeat step 4 to add another branched fringe, adjusting the length as desired.

6 After adding the fringe, sew through the beadwork to exit between the two end rows of 10ºs. Pick up a disk or flower bead and a 15º, and stitch it to the end of the band **[fig. 5]**. Retrace the thread path a few times, and end the thread (Basics).

Tip Your base may be a bit loose as you stitch, but as you add the second layer, use slightly tighter tension to snug up the bottom layer.

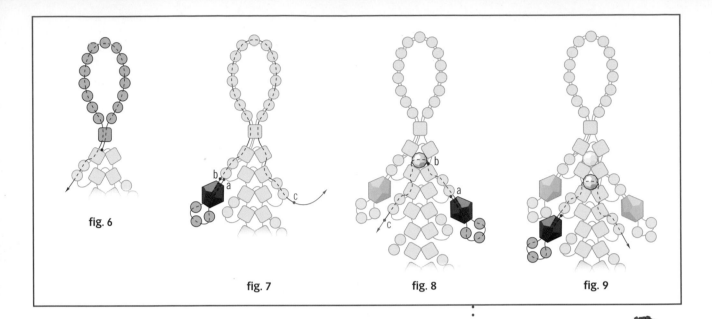

fig. 6

fig. 7

fig. 8

fig. 9

7 Using a 12-in. (30 cm) tail, pick up a 10º and enough 15ºs to make a loop that will fit around the clasp bead. Sew back through the 10º in the band, and the next two edge 15ºs **[fig. 6]**.

8 Pick up a 3 mm bicone and three 15ºs. Skip the last three 15ºs, and sew back through the 3 mm bicone, creating a picot below the crystal **[fig. 7, a–b]**. Sew through the next two 15ºs, two 10ºs, the loop of 15ºs, the next three 10ºs, and the next two 15ºs **[b–c]**.

9 Pick up a 3 mm bicone and three 15ºs. Skip the last three 15ºs, and sew back though the 3 mm bicone, creating a picot below the crystal. Sew through the next two 15ºs and the next 10º **[fig. 8, a–b]**. Pick up a 2 mm round crystal, and sew through the next two 10ºs and two 15ºs on the opposite side of the band **[b–c]**.

10 Repeat step 9 **[fig. 9]** to embellish both edges and the center of the band. When you reach the clasp bead, don't add the 2 mm crystal under the flower, but continue adding the crystal embellishment along the edges.

Featured necklace
4 mm, 3 mm, and 2 mm
   crystals: Vintage Rose
10º cylinders: matte metallic
   khaki iris
15º seed beads: gold-lined
   rainbow black diamond

Design option
4 mm bicone crystals: Light
   Colorado Topaz
3 mm bicone crystals: Garnet
8º cylinders: lined light topaz AB
11º cylinders: matte metallic
   olive green

COLORS

Design Option

Although the necklace ingredients make a lovely petite bracelet, you can stitch a slightly bolder version (shown here) using 8º cylinders instead of 10ºs, 11º cylinders instead of 15º seed beads, 4 mm bicones instead of 3 mms, and 3 mm bicones instead of 2 mm rounds.

This dramatic necklace with its
lily centerpiece and spiraling rope has lush layers
of texture and color throughout.

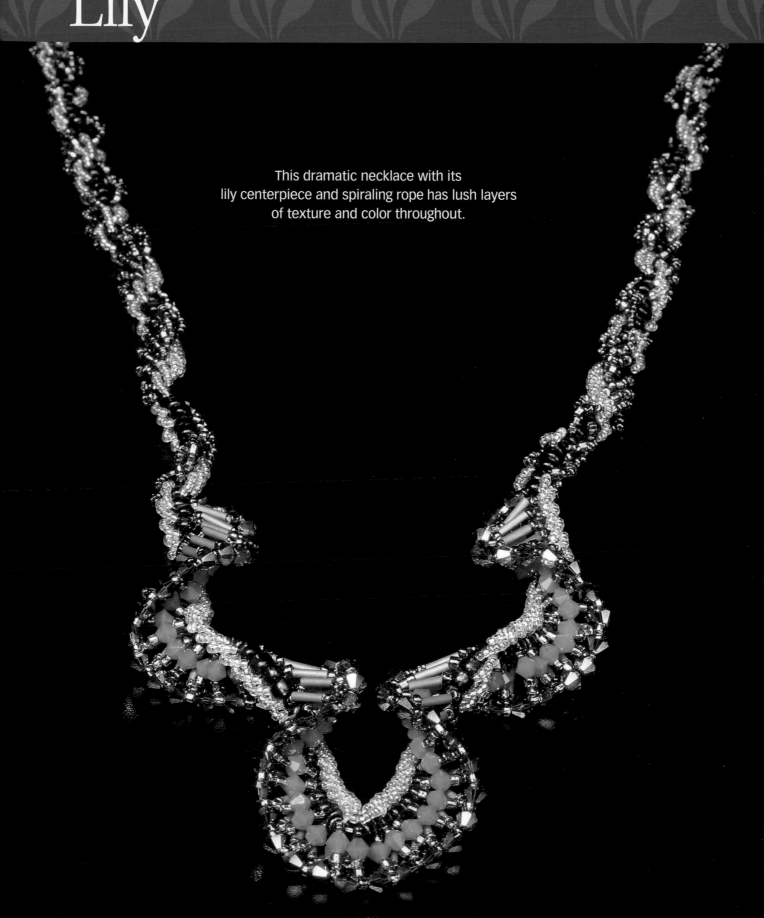

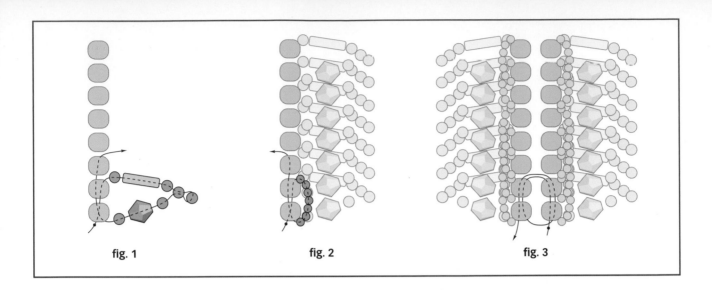

fig. 1 fig. 2 fig. 3

MATERIALS

For a 26-in. (66 cm) necklace

- 10 g 6 mm bugle beads
- 4 mm bicone crystals:
  64 color A
  67 color B
- 10 g 6º seed beads
- 25–30 g 11º seed beads
- 20–25 g 15º seed beads
- Clasp
- 2 jump rings
- Fireline 6 lb. test
- Beading needles, #12
- 2 pairs of pliers

Tip As you add the second row of loops, keep the first row of loops pushed to one side.

1 Attach a stop bead (Basics) to the end of 1 yd. (.9 m) of Fireline, leaving a 10-in. (25 cm) tail. Pick up 100 8º seed beads, and attach another stop bead.

2 On 2 yd. (1.8 m) of Fireline, sew through the first two 8ºs, leaving an 8-in. (20 cm) tail.

3 Pick up an 11º seed bead, a 6 mm bugle bead, and three 11ºs. Skip the last 11º, and sew back through the next 11º. Pick up

a

an 11º, a color A crystal, and an 11º. Sew through the two 8ºs your thread exited again, and continue through the next 8º **[fig. 1]**. Push the loop to the right.

4 Repeat step 3 32 times, each time pushing the new loop to the right.

5 Continue making loops, but pick up five 11ºs per stitch, until you reach the end of the base. End and add thread as needed (Basics).

6 On 2 yd (1.8 m) of Fireline, sew through the first two 8ºs.

7 Pick up seven 15ºs, sew through the two 8ºs your thread just exited again, and continue through the next 8º in the base **[fig. 2]**. Push the loop to the right next to the first row of loops.

8 Repeat step 7 until you reach the end of the base, ending and adding thread as needed, and saving one tail at the start of the large spiral end.

9 Repeat steps 1–8 to make a second spiral rope, but push the loops to the left instead of to the right.

10 Place the two spiral ropes next to each other on your work surface, and, using the tail from step 8, stitch the two end 8ºs on each side together **[fig. 3 and photo a]**. End the tail.

11 Using 2 yd. (1.8 m) of Fireline, sew into the beadwork on one spiral, exiting an 8º at the transition between the seed bead spirals and the bugle spiral. Pick up a color B 4 mm crystal, an 11º, and a B, and sew through the point 11º on the end bugle stitch **[photo b]**, leaving an 8-in. (20 cm) tail.

12 Pick up a B, and sew through the next point 11º **[photo c]**. Repeat, connecting all the points on one side of the spiral, then continue on through the second spiral **[photo d]**. Continue until all the bugle stitches are connected.

13 To connect the inner spirals, exit the 13th 11º along the outer edge of the large spiral. Pick up an 11º, a B, an 11º, a B, and an 11º, and sew through the corresponding 11º on the opposite spiral. Sew back through the beads just added, the 13th 11º on the spiral, and the next A and 11º.

14 Repeat step 12 twice, but pick up only an 11º, an A, and an 11º. Repeat step 12, and end the tails. Sew through the beadwork to exit the first loop of 15ºs on one rope, with the needle facing the center of the necklace. Pick up a 15º, and sew into the first loop of 15ºs on the other rope **[photo e]**.

15 Remove the stop bead from one of the 10-in. (25 cm) tails from step 1. Pick up seven 11ºs, and sew through the first 11º picked up to form a loop. Sew through the 11ºs again, skipping every other 11º so the loops form a square shape **[photo f]**. Retrace the thread path, and end the thread. Repeat on the other end.

16 Open a jump ring (Basics), and attach half the clasp to the loop. Repeat on the other end.

Design option

This necklace looks stunning with a deep V neckline, and you'll find it's very adaptable to match your favorite evening wear. This version features an organic colorway of cool greens, grays, and violet.

Curved Branch

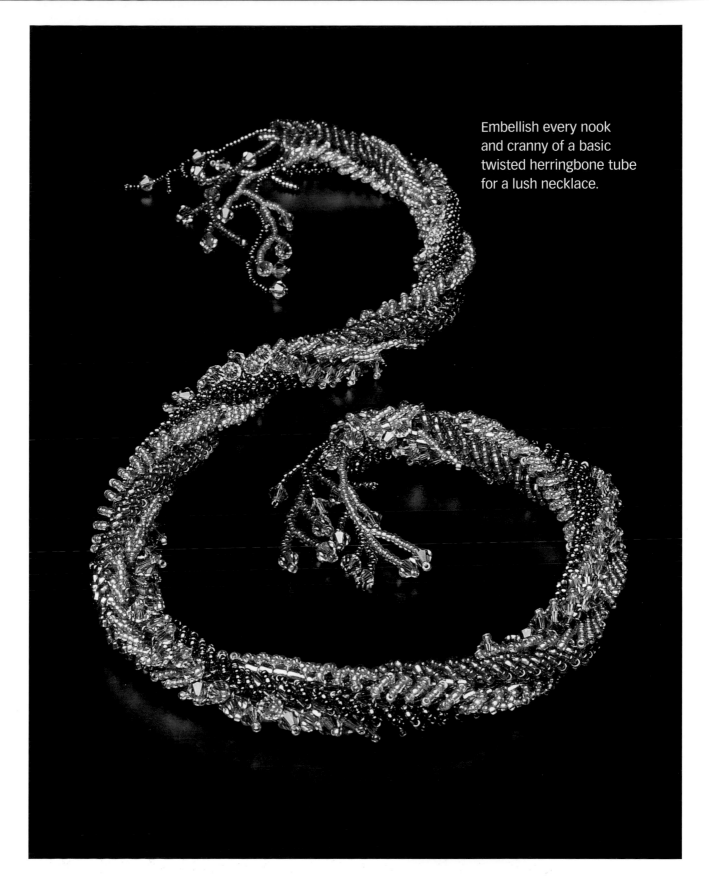

Embellish every nook
and cranny of a basic
twisted herringbone tube
for a lush necklace.

BASICS

For easy reference, all of the basic techniques used throughout
the projects are reviewed in the following pages.

Basics

Adding thread

To add a thread, sew into the beadwork several rows prior to the point where the last bead was added. Weave through the beadwork, following the existing thread path. Tie a few half-hitch knots between beads, and exit where the last stitch ended.

Ending thread

To end a thread, weave back into the beadwork, following the existing thread path and tying two or three half-hitch knots between beads as you go. Change directions as you weave so the thread crosses itself. Sew through a few beads after the last knot, and trim the thread.

Stop bead

Use a stop bead to secure beads temporarily as you begin stitching. Choose a bead that is distinct from the beads in your project. String the stop bead, and sew through it again in the same direction. For extra security, sew through it again.

Half-hitch knot

Pass the needle under the thread between two beads. A loop will form as you pull the thread through. Cross back over the thread between the beads, sew through the loop, and pull gently to draw the knot into the beadwork.

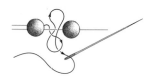

Peyote stitch—flat even-count

1 Pick up an even number of beads **[a–b]**. These beads will shift to form the first two rows.

2 To begin row 3, pick up a bead, skip the last bead strung in the previous step, and sew back through the next bead **[b–c]**. For each stitch, pick up a bead, skip a bead in the previous row, and sew through the next bead, exiting the first bead strung **[c–d]**. The beads added in this row are higher than the previous rows and are referred to as "up-beads."

3 For each stitch in subsequent rows, pick up a bead, and sew through the next up-bead in the previous row **[d–e]**. To count peyote stitch rows, count the total number of beads along both straight edges.

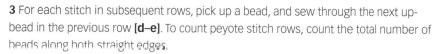

Peyote stitch—flat odd-count

Odd-count peyote is the same as even-count peyote, except for the turn on odd-numbered rows, where the last bead of the row can't be attached in the usual way because there is no up-bead to sew through.

Work the traditional odd-row turn as follows:

1 Begin as for flat even-count peyote, but pick up an odd number of beads. Work row 3 as in even-count, stopping before adding the last two beads.

2 Work a figure-8 turn at the end of row 3: Pick up the next-to-last bead (#7), and sew through #2, then #1 **[a–b]**. Pick up the last bead of the row (#8), and sew through #2, #3, #7, #2, #1, and #8 **[b–c]**.

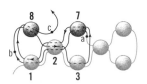

You can work this turn at the end of each odd-numbered row, but this edge will be stiffer than the other. Instead, in subsequent odd-numbered rows, pick up the last bead of the row, then sew under the thread bridge immediately below. Sew back through the last bead added to begin the next row.

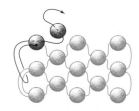

Basics

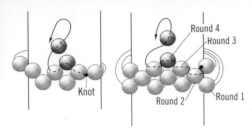

Tubular peyote stitch

Tubular peyote stitch follows the same stitching pattern as flat peyote, but instead of sewing back and forth, you work in rounds.

1 Start with an even number of beads in a ring.

2 Sew through the first bead in the ring. Pick up a bead, skip a bead in the ring, and sew through the next bead. Repeat to complete the round.

3 You need to step up to be in position for the next round. Sew through the first bead added in round 3. Pick up a bead, and sew through the second bead in round 3. Repeat to achieve the desired length.

Circular peyote stitch

Circular peyote is also worked in continuous rounds like tubular peyote, but the rounds stay flat and radiate outward from the center as a result of increases or using larger beads. If the rounds do not increase, the beadwork will become tubular.

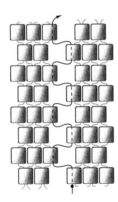

Zipping up or joining

To zip up (join) two sections of a flat peyote piece invisibly, match up the two end rows and zigzag through the up-beads on both ends.

Opening and closing plain loops, jump rings, and earring findings

1 Hold a loop or a jump ring with two pairs of pliers.

2 To open the loop or jump ring, bring the tips of one pair of pliers toward you, and push the tips of the other pair away from you. Reverse the steps to close.

Making a plain loop

1 Using chainnose pliers, make a right-angle bend approximately ¼ in. (6 mm) from the end of the wire.

2 Grip the tip of the wire with roundnose pliers. Press downward slightly, and rotate the wire into a loop. The closer to the tip of the pliers you work, the smaller the loop will be.

3 Let go, then grip the loop at the same place on the pliers, and keep turning to close the loop.

Making a wrapped loop

1 Using chainnose pliers, make a right-angle bend approximately 1¼ in. (3.2 cm) from the end of the wire.

2 Position the jaws of the roundnose pliers in the bend.

3 Curve the short end of the wire over the top jaw of the pliers.

4 Reposition the pliers so the lower jaw fits snugly in the loop. Curve the wire downward around the bottom jaw of the pliers. This is the first half of a wrapped loop.

5 To complete the wraps, grasp the top of the loop with chainnose pliers.

6 Wrap the wire around the stem two or three times. Trim the excess wire, and gently press the cut end close to the wraps with chainnose pliers.

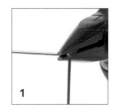

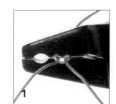

Crimping

Use crimping pliers and crimp beads to secure the ends of flexible beading wire:

1 Position the crimp bead in the notch closest to the handle of the crimping pliers. Hold the wires apart to make sure one wire is on each side of the dent, and squeeze the pliers to compress the crimp bead.

2 Position the crimp bead in the notch near the tip of the pliers with the dent facing the tips. Squeeze the pliers to fold the crimp in half. Tug on the wires to make sure the crimp is secure.

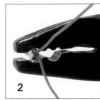

Other stitches used in the projects

You'll find step-by-step instructions for each of these techniques within the project instructions. Some projects use modified versions of the stitches.

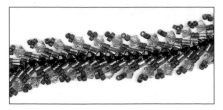

Flat herringbone stitch

The distinctive pattern of herringbone stitch (sometimes called Ndebele herringbone) places pairs of beads side by side and tilting in opposite directions, creating a ribbed look reminiscent of woven herringbone fabric.

Used in Featherweight (p. 80)

Spiral rope

This easy stitch features loops that embellish a core rope of beads. It lends itself to lots of variations as you change bead sizes and colors and the lengths of the loops.

Used in Lily (p. 83)

Netting

This is a naturally stretchy stitch that can be worked and embellished in many ways. Picking up a different number of beads in each stitch can vary the look dramatically.

Used in Queen (p. 18), Courtly (p. 23), Promenade (p. 29), Starlight (p. 42), Coquette (p. 48), XOXO (p. 57), Bright Lights (p. 62), Clusters (p. 70), Tide Pool (p. 78)

Twisted tubular herringbone

This stitch has a pattern similar to flat herringbone, but it is worked in rounds instead of back and forth. The twist is the result of a modified step-up.

Used in Curved Branch (p. 87)

Chevron chain

This is a lacy stitch that connects open triangles or rings of beads.

Used in Princess (p. 16), Lattice (p. 34), Antique Lace (p. 36), Metropolitan (p. 52)

Fringe

Fringe can be the main technique used to shape a piece (as in the Crown Jewels bracelet) or used as embellishment to another stitch (as in the Fairy Dust project).

Used in Crown Jewels (p. 14), Victoria (p. 26), Fairy Dust (p. 39), Featherweight (p. 80), Curved Branch (p. 87)

Right-angle weave

In this stitch, sometimes abbreviated as RAW, one stitch equals one square, with one bead on each side of the square.

Used in Majesty (p. 20), Fairy Dust (p. 39), Cubist (p. 54), Sputnik (p. 60), Cages (p. 65)

Daisy chain

This stitch is a close relative of right-angle weave. In its most basic form, the stitch has a square shape, and the thread travels in a circle to make each stitch; a bead in the center turns the square into a daisy.

Used in Clusters (p. 70)

About the Author

ANNA ELIZABETH DRAEGER has been designing beaded jewelry and accessories for nearly 20 years. Her first encounter with crystals in a bead shop in Woodstock, New York, has blossomed into a lasting passion she shares through her beaded creations.

Anna is an associate editor at *Bead&Button* magazine and author of the magazine's online column "Ask Anna." She also designs and sells beading kits and teaches beading at several venues in the U.S. and abroad. In 2009, Anna was named an ambassador for the Create Your Style with Crystallized Swarovski Elements program, an exclusive worldwide network of designers who are passionate about and prolific in using these Austrian crystal beauties in their projects and as they teach.

Anna lives in southeastern Wisconsin with her two sons.

Product sources
There's nothing like seeing all of the beautiful crystal colors and other beads in person, so please support your local store as you shop for project materials. Most bead stores carry an assortment of Crystallized Swarovski Elements. Online sources are another alternative. For more information on Create Your Style with Crystallized Swarovski Elements designs, products, events, and more, visit the Web site: create-your-style.com

Acknowledgments
I could not make what I make without the availability of beautiful beading materials. The Swarovski company continues to amaze me with innovative products in fabulous colors, and working with the Swarovski people has been a great experience for me. I am grateful for the support of the Create Your Style with Crystallized Swarovski Elements program while writing this book and designing the projects for it, and I am honored to be an ambassador for the program.

One of the most rewarding parts of my journey through life is the number of amazing women (and several men) who have taken my classes. The time I have spent chatting with and listening to these wonderful people makes what I do so worthwhile to me.

My family and friends are an unending source of encouragement, and I could not keep doing what I do without them. My children have been my constant joy, and I am so blessed to have them. I hope in this life I am able to give to others a bit of what the wonderful people in my life have given to me.

Big thanks to the Kalmbach team: Mary Wohlgemuth, Julia Gerlach, Lisa Bergman, Kellie Jaeger, and Bill Zuback.